NOT SO FAST

A GRAND TOUR OF EUROPE

AT A MID-LIFE PACE

For Carol and Marie!
Hope you love reading
our book! Peace—
Phebe Dale Hanson
Joan Murphy Pride

"Never be in a hurry, do everything quietly and in a calm spirit. Do not lose your inward peace for anything whatsoever even if your whole world seems upset."
                                        —St. Francis de Sales

"Always get the good out of every single day."
                                        —Anne Stanchina Murphy

"Think you've got life all figured out?
Not so fast."

                                        —Bonnie Hiatt

NOT SO FAST

A GRAND TOUR OF EUROPE
AT A MID-LIFE PACE

Phebe Dale Hanson
and
Joan Murphy Pride

NODIN PRESS

ACKNOWLEDGEMENTS

To Joan's and Phebe's family and friends who read earlier versions of this book and to those who gave us the use of their vacation homes, everlasting thanks:

Dennis Murphy Anderson, Carol Bly,
Jill Breckenridge/John Fenn, Judith Guest,
Patricia Hampl, Rolf Hanson/Ann Sundberg,
Carol Heen, Linda Heen, Pamela Holt,
Louise Irving, Leah Lawrence, Howard and Jody Mohr,
Erik and Mary Riese, Marly Rusoff/Mihai Radelescu,
Norton Stillman, Faith Sullivan,
Cary Waterman, Charlie Boone.
Phebe thanks the Bush Foundation for its generous
financial support.

Layout and cover design: John Toren

Nodin Press is a division of Micawbers, Inc.
530 N Third Street
Suite 120
Minneapolis, Minnesota
55401

To the memory of my parents
David and Hildur Dale

—P. D. H.

For my son and friend,
Dennis Murphy Anderson

—J. M. P.

Table of Contents

INTRODUCTION

After our kids were grown and gone, we traveled for two months through Europe the way we should have in our 20's, without guides, baggage carriers, rigid schedules or lots of money.

The trip was occasioned by Phebe, a college English professor, winning a Bush Literary Grant. It included a year off and travel money for research in Norway. Joan pretended to be happy for her but she was seething with jealousy. She was a writer and partner in an advertising agency with two lovable but chauvinistic men who wished that she would just shut up and make the coffee. So she gave herself a grant. She quit, took a year off to write, and said to Phebe:

"As long as you're going to Norway, why not stop off along the way in Amsterdam, Brussels, Paris, Lausanne, the Cinque Terra, Rome, Florence, Venice, the Dolomites, Munich, Frankfurt, the Romantic Road and the Rhine Cruise. And I'll go with you. Actually, I don't want to go to Norway but I'll be your boon companion all the rest of the way."

And so the next spring, off we went. We argued and laughed and wrote furiously in our journals about all the great things: the cathedrals, the castles, the museums and finding Joan's family in Italy. And we wrote about the small moments: the early morning smell of bread baking in Brussels, the glowing candles in front of the Virgin at a convent in Rome where Lutheran Phebe turned Catholic for a week, and a rainy day in Paris made glorious when the sun shone in through those incredible windows in Ste.Chapelle.

And we wrote about our lives too, because everything we saw reminded us of home.

NOT SO FAST

A GRAND TOUR OF EUROPE

AT A MID-LIFE PACE

1. A YEAR TO GET READY
Our Minneapolis-Montevideo letters

September 3

Dear Joan,

What a relief to be moved to Montevideo at last. I never could have done it without you. That mover who kept telling us about his heart attack and asking me why I needed so many books made me feel very guilty. I feel guilty enough about leaving St. Paul for a year when I'm supposed to be getting a divorce. Besides, I feel guilty about leaving my children. Oh, I know they're grown and settled into school and careers. Wouldn't you think I could leave them? No, I still think they need me close by at all times. How are they going to get along without me?

So what have I done since I moved in? I've actually set up my IBM computer, which has been languishing in the carton since I bought it last May. I've also set up a schedule for myself, beginning with devotions. My father would be so proud of me. Actually, I'm not reading all these little books from any great concern for my spiritual life, but to calm me down. I'm so nervous at the prospect of being here alone for a whole year with no schedule, just this big writing project. The responsibility is overwhelming. I guess when I applied for that huge grant I never really expected to get it. Now miracle of miracles, they're actually sending me money every month. Not to mention money for my computer and the travel stipend that will send me to Norway.

Your nervous friend, Phebe

September 8

My dear Phebe,

Well, we got you to Montevideo, but I am still sore and in shock from carrying furniture and heavy boxes up all those stairs.

I've got to tell you I've been horribly jealous of your year off, and I've been thinking. Every day we have is a "grant." The dumb way I spend my days has been the result of my own lack of long-range planning. I thought why can't I give myself a grant, too, the time to do whatever I want?

Well, I told Bob I was quitting the agency. You know how I've hated it, all the employee and client problems, the acres of headaches. But I only want to quit the agency, not Bob, too. In spite of our fights, I do still love him and find him sexy, intense, funny, intelligent, forgetful, hideously messy, with enough energy to light the Pentagon. An interesting husband, an exhausting business partner. I was worried about telling him I wanted out. Well, I needn't have worried. Bob seems as relieved to have me leave as I will be to be gone.

I don't know what I'll do yet. Write, I suppose. I bought a new computer, a Mac. So easy to use. And I want to travel. I know you have travel money to go to Norway as part of your grant. How about going to some other countries, too? And I'll go with you.

Love, Joan

September 15

Dear Joan,

I've been spending some of my grant money for a good cause. I've been reading articles in the local newspaper bemoaning the fact that several downtown businesses have closed. So I personally have been doing my best to keep downtown Monte afloat. I try to spread my business around, too, from the restaurants, to the craft shops, to the clothing stores. I've taken to buying books from the Good News Bookstore, a place full of Bibles, Bible commentaries, and devotional literature.

I'm thrilled you've decided to give yourself a grant year and even more thrilled that you've decided to travel with me.

4

I was getting nervous about traveling alone. I laughed when you suggested all those other countries besides Norway.

Now I have a proposal. How about making our travel arrangements at the local travel agency to help the economy here? You could come visit me (I'm already lonesome for you—yes, I admit it) and we could confer with the lovely women who run the agency. That would be kind, like the Bible tells us to be. But Catholics don't believe in reading the Bible. Your pope and priests read it for you and tell you what to think about it. Don't get mad. I can't help the things my father taught me.

Kindly, Phebe

September 19

Dear Phebe,

I do worry about you with all that grant money and 139 miles from my strict eye. Why not have me declared your guardian? I would be so fair and generous. I don't know why you go crazy every time I bring it up.

I am ignoring your anti-Catholic remarks. First, because I, as a true Christian, was taught to turn the other cheek. Second, because I truly pity the paucity of your education about THE ONE TRUE CHURCH. And third, because I know you aren't really a biased person. Actually, your insults pale beside a remark one of your teacher friends made to me at your going-away party. She asked me if I was a "recovering Catholic." And to think I didn't even know I was sick.

I can understand your concern for your new home town, but you go too far when you say we must arrange our trip there, a small town with 5,000 people and one travel agency. Remember, I still live in Minneapolis, a huge city with thousands of qualified agents and hundreds of full-service agencies. Oh well, it's your trip so we'll plan our trip in Monte.

I'll come, I'll come at the earliest light of dawning that I can manage.

Your obedient pal, Joan

September 26

Dear Joan,

Your proposal to become my guardian certainly rang a
bell. Did I ever tell you about my stepmother's diabolical plan
in 1948, when I took a year off college to teach in a one-room
country school? She was enraged when she heard I'd signed
a contract without consulting her or my father. She'd always
been firmly convinced I didn't know how to handle money.
So she wrote to her lawyer and asked him to tell her what the
procedure was to have herself declared my legal guardian, so
my pay checks could be sent directly to her.

How do I know this? Well, a few years before my father
died, he came over to my house with a big brown box of
mementos—letters, diaries, school papers, report cards—from
my childhood and youth. Tucked inside one of the piles of
letters was a letter of reply from the lawyer. I'm sure my father
didn't know the letter was there. Or maybe, now that I think of
it, he was finally letting me know that it wasn't his fault she'd
tried to get control of my money. The lawyer said that since I
was only 20, she was already my legal guardian. Back then you
weren't considered of legal age until you were twenty-one.

She wrote to the country superintendent, asking that my
pay check be mailed home. But the superintendent refused my
stepmother's request. I got the lavish sum of $200 a month,
big bucks in 1948. I spent my first pay check foolishly, just as
my stepmother had predicted, on new winter clothes. Monte
was the nearest town with a department store, so that's where
we went. I had no car, didn't even know how to drive, so
the farmer's wife with whom I boarded, took me. Monte
seemed like such a glamorous town then, with a flourishing
downtown. What has happened?

Oh, maybe I *should* hand over all my financial affairs to
you. But do you really want that responsibility? You'd have to
do my income taxes too. I'm dreading that chore, because John
has faithfully done them all these 30 years.

Love, Phebe

October 1

Hi Phebe pal,

I opened a separate bank account today to save for our trip. I trust my free lance work will pick up soon, so I won't have to siphon the whole trip out of housekeeping. Bob is worse than you are about money. He'd probably never even notice. What can you expect from a man who calls money from the Instant Cash Machines—lucky bucks?

This is the third time I've saved money for a European trip. So now I feel like I'm being given a third chance and the number 3 is lucky, right? I'm feeling guilty about leaving Bob. I told him that the trip would be two weeks, but now the Must-Sees have expanded to four, and it may end up being six weeks. I feel guilty, but being Catholic, my primary emotion is guilt anyway. This trip will make the feeling worthwhile.

Must quit. The fence man is here. He will tell me how much it will cost to change our back yard into a Large Outdoor Toilet for the dog, which could save me an average of seven walks a day. Ancient Arnold has many adorable qualities, his tiny bladder not being one of them.

Love, Joan

October 7

Dear Joan,

Another day has gone by and no letter from you. What's the point of your beautiful new Mac? I myself am still writing by hand or on my old typewriter. Both are faster than getting embroiled in the IBM. You know how I love to underline. It's a trait I inherited from my father, who always ended up underlining every word in his carefully written-out sermons. I asked him once why he did that. "For emphasis," he said. "It's all important—every word."

You'll be amazed to hear I've taken to attending church quite regularly. Last Sunday at the coffee hour, a woman rushed up to talk to me, saying she'd heard I was a writer and wanted advice on her writing project. After her husband died, she decided to research every occupant of every Chippewa County cemetery. She figured it would take her the rest of her life to finish. Is this what I have to look forward to as an unmarried woman—searching for meaning in the lives of the deceased?

Love, Phebe

October 9

My dear friend Phebe,

The Lord is looking out for me a little. You weren't home when I called just now so I figure I saved about $18 towards Europe. I tried to call because I haven't really had time to write. My dad is in the hospital. He felt quite out of breath last weekend so sister Pat took him to the emergency room and they admitted him. I trust that was more because of his age—almost 94 now—than his condition. It seems strange to see him lying about. I think of him as indestructible and eternal, you know. Last winter I got dozens of calls from friends and neighbors who had seen him up shoveling snow off the roof of his house. I beg him not to do this. He fell off once last year. Thank God, the snow was deep.

Anyway, I know you love to get mail. Perhaps you will pick this little letter out of your mailbox when you come home tired and cold some evening, exhausted from visiting cemeteries and spreading money rapidly and carelessly about southwestern Minnesota.

I'm glad you're coming to spend some time in Minneapolis next week. It's hard to plan and re-plan our Grand Tour on long distance calls, although they must be delighting Ma Bell. I don't want to leave any part of our trip to chance. I want it to be the most-researched, mapped-out, shopped-for, fought-over, discussed trip to Europe of any in history since D-Day in World War II.

Love, Joan

October 13

Dear Joan,

I'm sorry to hear your dad's in the hospital, but I'm sure he'll soon be home, as full of life as ever. I've never known any

8

one who seemed more alive than he. What a miracle he is, still so interested in the world at 94. Such a good model for us as we go into "the youth of our old age," as someone once called our fifties and sixties. Why is it I feel like I just graduated from college and the whole bright world lies before me? Maybe it does.

I've gone back to Weight Watchers. Last night our leader was eloquent about techniques to keep from eating too much. She told us to sit down at the table with our best china and silver.

Light a candle and breathe deeply. Eat slowly, savoring each mouthful. Afterwards, take a long hot bubble bath. I've tried all that, but I've never met a bubble bath that could rival a Snickers.

Now I shall close. Write back. That's what I always said to my pen pal in Sault Saint Marie. I used to write her when I was in seventh grade. Did you ever have a pen pal? I suppose not. You were too busy dating. Oh, you sexy Catholic girls. We Lutherans always envied you. Necking in the back seats of cars, never having to worry about Jesus watching. "Do nothing you would not want to be doing when Jesus comes," my father used to tell us. But you Catholics could neck away, then go to confession and forget about it.

Love, Phebe

November 15

Phebe dear,

I've been meaning to write to you every day since you left to go back to Monte. It was so great of you to stay nearly two weeks with me. I really needed the company and the help. I just can't seem to do anything since dad's funeral but sit around and brood.

How little I understood what was going on in my life. Do all adult children feel this way as their parents age, need help, and die? I thought I was the important one, a caregiver Dad couldn't get along without, especially during the time Mom was sick and after she died. I never once stopped to think how much I needed them to be there.

Now that I'm no one's child, I look in the mirror and see an old woman.

I was still leaning, still dependent, as he was dying. I told him all about my ideas for a new life, a new career. Should I go back to school to get another degree? Should I look for a job in community service? What do you think, Dad? He said, "What should you be? Be happy."

Be happy. Well, I'm trying. But it's really hard without him.

Love, Joan

November 20

Dear Joan,

I'm glad I was staying with you when you got news of your father's death. And he was too young to die. The older I get, the younger each age seems. When is a good time to die? My answer, of course, would be never. I can barely imagine a time when I'll have lost my curiosity, my interest in life, my desire to know how everything turns out.

Your father, even though many would say he had lived long enough, still had such a zest for life. I'm sure he had his down times, but he seemed to me like a man who'd made up his mind to be happy, no matter what trials came his way. He was so patient with your mother all those years. Not many men his age would be able to accept that kind of care giving with such calmness. It's thanks to him she never had to go into a nursing home.

After the funeral you told me that people kept saying what a long wonderful life your dad had lived. As if that meant you shouldn't be feeling any grief. You were fed up, you said, with people telling you how you should feel. There is something disgusting about the way we Americans often psychologize and categorize all human emotions. So many think they're instant shrinks if they've read a few pop psychology books, including me. Let me know if I get too insufferable with all my self -help books.

On second thought, don't let me know. You're already taking far too seriously your belief that somehow because your name is Joan and my long-gone sister's name was Jo Anne, you have been sent as her re-incarnation to give me sisterly advice. Didn't I ever explain to you that Jo Anne was sweet and mild-mannered and thoughtful? She would never try to take control of my money nor give me any advice whatsoever.

Love, Phebe

December 1

My dear Phebe,

I am taking Macintosh in hand to write to you today. Anything rather than call which I am itching to do and which I cannot. I just paid my AT&T bill and we could have had three nights in a Paris hotel for what it cost. Oh well, I think I'll go call you. I've been worried that you were somewhere near South Dakota in the Old Dodge Ark and couldn't get home.

Today I met with a new client and he was quite nice, considering that I was 20 minutes late. The entire time he was giving me directions on the phone I was drawing little daggers and not paying a bit of attention. I hate getting directions over the phone. Actually, my sense of direction is non-existent, which bodes ill for Europe. I trust you can read a map. Funny the things you don't know about an old friend.

I do know you were smart in school, but so what? What was the point? Are you rich today? No. Neither, sadly, am I. What was the point of always having your hand up first in grade school? We would be so perfect as rich people. We wouldn't have to plot and plan our trip so carefully to save a sou here, a lire there. My sister is settling Dad's estate and keeps trying to talk to me about money. I can't bear to think about it. Not yet.

I hope you are at this very moment writing me a funny letter.

Love, Joan

December 6

Dear Joan,

How can I write you a funny letter when I am still plagued by fear and guilt and indecision: fear of the IBM, fear of being alone the rest of my life, guilt at leaving my grown children and darling granddaughter to fend for themselves in the wicked city, guilt that I'm not writing more poems, indecision about whether or not to file for divorce.

I've tried to take care of the first fear by covering the IBM with a prayer shawl and a DO NOT DISTURB sign from the office supply store where yesterday I also bought correction fluid and Pilot Razor Point pens. Am I not in trouble?

Yes, I understand why it's hard for you to think about your dad's money. Of course, I never had to deal with that, because I never saw any of my dad's money, if indeed there was any. My half-brother and stepmother handled everything and I was never consulted. I would have liked my real mother's wedding dishes and silverware and the contents of her trunk from Sweden but I never dared ask. Wonder where they are? When I asked my half-brother he said, "Oh, that stuff was all hauled to the dump."

Love, Phebe

December 9

Dear Phebe,

The best present you can give me this year START SAVING MONEY FOR EUROPE. We will get deeply into financial talks when you arrive for the holidays in a couple weeks. Until then, please quit buying things like luggage. You could end up with three or four bags and backpacks, all of them wrong.

I beg you to remember that when I fed your psychological data into Mind Probe on my Macintosh, your personality profile clearly stated that you often look for "magic solutions" to your everyday problems. This is not going to butter any pommes de terre in Europe. Cold hard dollars are what they're looking for.

Your friend, Joan

December 13

Dear Joan,

Getting that Mind Probe from your Macintosh infuriated me. To think a machine would dare to say I seek "magic solutions." Of course, it did occur to me to wonder what you'd told the machine to make it come up with all those answers. I'm not stupid. I know those machines can't think for themselves.

But I guess I do rely on magic solutions, like draping the computer with a prayer shawl, hoping the vibrations of ancient mystics' prayers will somehow make it possible for me to figure out how to type a simple sentence on the damn machine without getting a response that could have come straight from my father were he not safely in his grave: "BAD COMMAND! BAD COMMAND!" Sounds suspiciously like what he used to say to me when I acted like a brat: "YOU'VE BEEN MEAN FROM THE DAY YOU WERE BORN."

Love, Phebe

December 16

Dear Phebe,

I have been thinking about going to a weight class too, because something has to change. Last night I dreamt my skin split here and there like old car upholstery.

I was horribly embarrassed by Arnold the Dog when I picked him up today at the vet's. He pretended never to have laid eyes on me before, not so much unfriendly as just too, too blasé to return my effusive greetings. Then, after I paid my bill and was about to leave, he lifts his leg and wets all over their appointment desk. Now Mr. Two-Faced is right behind my chair where he has been the entire day, fawning over me and acting like I'm his greatest chum and he's the world's sweetest dog. He doesn't fool me with his great brown eyes and silky, sweet face. He sold me out twice this very day.

I am enclosing some information on a one-day course in January for your IBM computer at the U of M. It sounds good and basic. So this course could get you going. What say you? You can't keep a shawl on your computer forever with a DO NOT DISTURB sign on top. We all know who's really disturbed there.

Write soon as I miss you like anything, dear friend.

—Joan

December 20

Dear Joan,

Even though I'm all alone as Christmas approaches, I've decided to pretend I'm still in the bosom of my family. I bought a new Advent wreath from—where else?—the Good News Bookstore. I also bought a miniature creche set from Bavaria. Miniatures are the way for me to go now since I seem to be living a rootless, wandering life, without husband, forgotten by children and friends. A little self-pity never hurt anyone, did it?

Speaking of miniatures, I ran across this headline in the Minneapolis paper yesterday in the Monte library, where I still go in the afternoons, ostensibly to do research, but actually to escape the sight of my prayer-shawled IBM. Here's the item, headline and all: "TINY BUDDHA CARVED. An amateur engraver has carved on bronze an image of the Buddha smaller than a sesame seed." To waste even more time so I won't have to think about the IBM, I've been fantasizing about crocheting little outfits for my miniature creche figures.

I've invited the kids to Monte. Maybe I'll call John and invite him too. Is it OK to invite your soon-to-be-ex for an overnight? Oh, why not. We're still a family, always will be, even though the kids are all grown up—Erik married and a father, Rolf teaching school and Leah a sophomore at the U. Do you find it just as hard to believe that Dennis is grown up?

Love, Phebe

January 15

My dear Phebe,

I trust I am not too late to wish you a very happy New Year. It was great having you here after Christmas but I fear we played the time away and didn't get enough done on our trip. Now we must get right into languages. I will brush up on French and you should start today to learn Italian and German. A very fair division of labor, if I do say so myself. The very thought of you trying to become fluent in both languages in four months makes me quite faint. Just do Italian.

I am busy today planning a birthday party for Dennis. We'll go down to Rochester and take dinner along with us. I wonder every day if Dennis is safe, is happy, is eating enough vegetables, is really and truly flossing. When will I quit worrying about him? He's just fine, loves what he's doing as creative director at the radio station, goes with a darling woman, a school teacher, and lives with Kevin who is heaven.

Why didn't any one tell us that motherhood is the job that never ends? Write quickly with the answer.

Love, Joan

January 19

Dear Joan,

Since I got back from the Cities and am once again all alone here in the hinterlands, I suppose you think I should have plenty of time to learn the languages you've chosen for me—Italian and German. But with my usual clever ability to find diversions from assigned tasks, I've taken to reading Thoreau. Remember his creed—Simplify! Simplify! Our shopping trips to find the perfect travel outfits were excessive, but since all the clothes I bought are still in the bags, with the price tags still on them, I can certainly weed out a few things in a suitably Thoreau-esque manner.

Now I'm thinking about what you said to me when we were shopping—NO FLASHY CLOTHES—because they would immediately brand us as American tourists and we'd be targets for terrorists. How did that stereotype get started anyhow, that Americans always wear flashy clothes? My closet is full of black clothes from teaching at MCAD where black is the school color.

Love, Phebe

February 10

My dear Phebe,

Now that you're gone, I have turned for companionship to my Mac and she is rewarding me with new tricks daily. I now have all my friends in a data base that tells me when they were born, what they had to eat last time at my house, what sizes I know, and most important of all—whether or not they sent me a Christmas card last year which indicates whether they will be getting one from me next year.

Bob's off on a ski trip and he's in heaven. The resort is putting him, for just a little more money than he would have to pay for a luxurious suite, right into a yurt. That's right, a yurt. He will be allowed to ski deep into the forest in the dead of night where he will lodge in what sounds like an old sheep-herder's wagon, complete with smoky wood stove, kerosene lamp and lumpy old sheep-herder's bed. He is so excited at the prospect of all this discomfort he is nearly swooning. As I am about Europe. Where are your plans? It is only 14 weeks away. Zut alors, what a trip we shall have.

Love, Joan

February 14

Dear Joan,

It was great to stay with you once more last week. Bob's a good sport not to complain about my frequent forays into your digs. Wish him a happy Valentine's Day from me.

Where are all my Europe plans you asked in your last letter. No hurry, I say, but I know it makes you nervous to hear that. Actually, I did put together an itinerary the other day. How about if we fly into Dublin, then train to Rosslare where we could board the ferry to Le Havre, only a short distance from Paris. Then from Paris we'd take excursions to Chartres and Fontainbleu. From Paris we'd go Eurail to Rome with day trips to Naples and Pompeii, then on to Florence and Venice and Bern, with a day excursion to Rheinfelden. I have in my hands a guide book that says it's a "medieval jewel" and that it "stirs the imagination." We certainly want our imaginations stirred, don't we?

Only a few months until we're there, dear friend.

Love, Phebe

February 20 Out in Chetek

Chere Phebe,

We will be in the City of Light in just over two months. Our next planning session should be on the final route. I don't understand why you want to start in Dublin but we can talk about it. I will come to Monte early in the week of March 3 and you can drive back with me for your birthday.

We're spending the week end in Chetek and Bob has gone into town on some errands, so I'm all alone here, deep in the forest and a mile from the closest neighbor. It's very quiet and spooky. Right before he left, Bob double-locked the back door with a dead bolt key—"just in case." As I imagine that the cast from "Deliverance" could be out there waiting on the woods and might descend on me now that I'm alone and easily push in the glass front door, it doesn't make me feel any safer.

Actually, I don't think of the country as peaceful. I think of it as miles from a really decent discount store.

Love, Joan

February 26

Dear Joan,

Less than a month until spring and I should be rejoicing, since we're that much closer to our Day of Departure. But the thought fills me with ever-increasing dread. What made me think I wanted to travel? What made me think I have the courage to fly over the Atlantic Ocean, I who can only swim side stroke?

I don't really mean it. Of course I'm going. If necessary, I'll force myself to leave this comfortable life in this quiet, safe town where I can leave the key in the ignition of my Dodge Monaco, confident that no one will steal it.

I went to Women's Bible Study this morning. Still in the book of Romans, where we've been since I started last fall. Several meetings had to be cancelled, due to bad weather. Our leader decided we needed an exhaustive review to remind us of "all the stuff we'd probably forgotten during all those blizzards." She wore us out with the review and then took off for California, first appointing another woman to take over. The new leader did very well, I thought. Moved us smartly along. But when the old leader came back, she felt it necessary to review all the chapters we'd covered in her absence, since she was concerned the new teacher might not have emphasized all the things she, our real teacher, considered important. At this rate we'll never get to my favorite passage in Romans—16: 1: "I commend unto you our sister Phebe who hath done many good works among you."

Love from your sister in Christ, Phebe

March 18

Dear Phebe,

I was thrilled to hear that you're living where you feel safe enough to leave the keys right in your old Dodge. With any luck at all, it will soon be stolen. Face it, Phebe. That car is too big for you. I remember the first time you drove up to my house. All I could see was the very top of your little head. I thought it was a precocious three-year-old driver come to call.

I loved your story of Bible study in Monte. My mother belonged to just such a group, the St. Joseph Study Club, for thirty years or more. Yes, to answer the question I can feel forming on your prejudiced Lutheran lips, Catholics ARE allowed to read the Bible. Encouraged, even.

I've been thinking about the money we're taking on our Grand Tour and I'm sure it will be enough. After all, despite what travel magazines say, I don't believe you have to be a millionaire to enjoy Europe. Where do the teachers from Spain stay when they visit Rome? Or the little bank tellers from Germany and Paris? We'll be fine, comfortable, and happy. Not flush but certainly not starving, either.

Don't be scared. Practice being brave a little each day and by the time we're flying, you shall be fearless, 39 days from now. Nothing will happen to you in Europe and anyway I will be there to take care of you. It's going to be wonderful. I just got two great walking tour books for Rome and Florence from Bob. I wish I'd had them two weeks ago when you were here. We could've spent the week poring over them together.

Love, Joan

March 24

Dear Joan,

Thanks for your letter trying to allay my fear of flying. What I'm worried about now is that our tickets haven't arrived yet. I called the travel agency to find out why, but I don't want you to worry. If anything goes amiss with the tickets, it will be my head that's on the block. Wherever did I come up with that expression? Must hark back to my childhood summer on Dahl's farm, where I stayed when my mother was so sick. Often I watched Mrs. Dahl—it seemed to be woman's work—hold chickens down by their legs on an old tree stump and chop off their heads. And yes, they did run around afterward for fortunately a very brief time.

I must sign off. The thought of those chickens has made me too nervous to continue. I'm filled with constant low-grade anxiety. Wake up every morning—sometimes in the middle of the night—thinking of all the things I haven't done this year in Monte—letters I haven't answered, books I haven't read, poems I haven't written up. What does "written up" mean anyway? When I was in the 8th grade I was tapped for the job of collecting Sacred Heart news for the neighboring town's newspaper. "I hear you're a smart girl," the editor said to me. "I'm sure you'll figure out a way to write it up." And I did write up a storm, because I got paid by the column inch. I wrote up local events in intricate detail so I'd get more money. But then my stepmother insisted it all had to go into the family coffers.

Have I told you about my first paying job before? Please don't tell me you've heard the same story many times. I figure not to worry about repeating myself because I figure you'll have forgotten that I've told it before.

Well, I'm not getting paid for this so I'll sign off the way I did then—30—

Love from your faithful reporter, Phebe

Easter

Dear Phebe,

I'm sending you Easter greetings a little early, as we are leaving for Yellowstone on Saturday for our big ski trip. I am very nervous about the week coming up, but I am trying to concentrate on the animals and the scenery and let the skiing recede to a small, terrified part of my brain. We will both downhill at Big Sky and lots of cross country through the park. Dennis should be in heaven. It's real cowboy country so he can wear his South Dakota hat and boots. I think I'll call and tell him so. Are your kids coming out for Easter? I guess I'll call you tonight.

I can afford to. Monte Travel called yesterday and they have found another company, same plane, to Amsterdam which will save me at least $50. Good old Monte Travel. As I have always said, use a small local travel agency. They really care about their customers.

Nothing much else new. I'm reading Mom's journal of one of her trips to Europe and I'd like to see some of the same sights. I think I'll take a copy of her writings along. Makes me sad—she sounded so young, so excited as she wrote this.

Hope there's a letter from you 'ere my return. I will return and with no parts broken or missing, won't I?

Love, Joan

April 15

Dear Joan,

Here I am back in Monte, glad to be "home," after those two weeks of Poets in the Schools residencies. Sure am grateful to you and Bob for all the love and attention you gave me after my back went out, especially for finding that wonderful chiropractor. I'm sure I'll be fine by our departure.

Several of my new-found Monte friends have asked me if, in light of (or should I say in dark of) our bombing Libya, we're still going ahead with our plans to travel. Are we not afraid of terrorists? "No more than I am of turbulence over the Atlantic Ocean," I always answer, speaking aloud my real fear in a vain attempt to exorcise it. I'm plunging ahead despite the bombing and the bad back. Today I went to the credit union and got my $2100 in travelers checks--$50 a day for 42 days.

People have been offering to pray for my back's healing. I am happy to let them. My new motto is to try anything that can't hurt and might help. I've come a long way since I was a student at Augsburg and found that a group of super-devout girls in my dorm were praying for me because I rarely came to evening devotions. Made me furious. Not any more. Now I'll take all the prayers I can get.

Prayerfully yours, Phebe

April 28

Dear Phebe,

Well, the house seems sad and lonely since you've been gone, the way it did when my darling only child went off to college. But it has finally quit snowing. Soon I will dress and go downtown to the – ugggghhhh – office for a client presentation of awards. I don't want to do this, but contrary to what Brenda Ueland told us, you do have to do things you don't want to do. Every day. Oftener if you're married.

I'm enclosing our Next To Last Grand Tour Itinerary on the off chance that you cannot read yours or that you have lost it in the welter of purchases with which you have returned to Monte.

I've spent the days reading my mother's journal of her trip to Europe. And also letters, one to my father from Paris that's nine pages long. She talks about going to the Follies and says,

"The girls wear nothing but a little belt around their waists. They're so lovely." She goes on to say she finds the show both beautiful and demeaning, a comment from a woman who both loved beauty and was an early feminist.

The most amazing thing. My wonderful new guide book has explicit directions for both the boat trip on the Rhine and the bus trip down the Romantic Road. And both of them are free or rather included in the price of our Eurail pass. We can easily fit them both in. What luck.

Enou, enou. That's Old English according to the crossword puzzle makers.

Love, Joan

2. UP IN THE AIR
What exactly is normal turbulence?

MAY 8

JOAN
(MINNEAPOLIS)

Departure Day: In his never-ending quest to Keep-Joan-Off-Guard, Bob is being truly wonderful. I had expected that he would be angry and I would trundle off to Europe with a heavy heart and burning stomach. Not so fast, those of you who feel you understand your man. Bob is being sweet and tender and as dear and charming as only he can be. So I will still leave for Europe with a heavy heart but for a different reason.

Last night Bob fixed a farewell dinner for me—steak, fettucine, asparagus, salad, strawberries and cream. We talked and made love and talked some more. It was a very tender night. It seems as though I hardly slept at all, already missing Bob so much, but that can't be true. About 4 am a terrific thunderstorm broke with wild lightning and groans of thunder, then buckets, hoses of water. The morning finally dawned clear but gray. Like my spirits.

Phebe just called, voice taut, to give me her latest packing changes and the exact route she will take to the airport in her old and very unreliable Dodge. She seems to think that I will be able to zip out on the freeways and find her should she not be in place when I arrive at the airport. To throw a spanner into the workings of fate, vis-á-vis the old Dodge, she will arrive at the airport quite early—10:30 am for a 1:15 pm flight.

I pack my bag and weigh it. Exactly 20 pounds just as Phebe and I have agreed will be the perfect weight. I know I will be buying lots of books, I always do, so the bag will get progressively heavier throughout Europe. To find out exactly how much I can carry, I try to remember how big my son was before it was impossible for me to carry him around. As Dennis was almost 10 pounds when he was born, I'm sure I remember being able to lug him about until he was fifty pounds or more. Of course, I was younger then. But I remember reading somewhere that women have an amazing ability to carry large loads long distances because of our hips or something. Another bit of the flotsam that floats through my brain, unproven and fragmented—instead of a first class grasp of something really important.

Finally, it's really time to leave and I go to say goodbye to the animals. Arnold, the Three-Legged Dog, looks sad but then he always does, even in his new red bandana collar. Delilah, the World's Oldest Living Cat, always the little helpmate, hides and I have to go crawling about looking under the beds and in the closets for her. She does this every time I go away, having a strong sense of the dramatic coupled with her feline ESP.

At the airport: We met Phebe and Leah for lunch. Phebe is so excited, red-cheeked and nervous. It's a joy to see her, she seems quite like a young girl. Bob and I are sad.

Bob continues to be wonderful and very supportive, helping me get on the plane and yet conveying strongly that he will miss me dreadfully. A perfect combination. He slips me an amulet as I go through the checkpoint. It's a calculator that turns dollars into many different foreign currencies and miles into kilometers. Very fancy, probably expensive and so thoughtful.

The first leg of our journey takes us to Chicago and either I've grown in the past year or they're making plane seats only for children these days. We're met in Chicago by a tiny little person who runs us two miles to the International Terminal through corridor after corridor, up and down stairs, until I think my lungs are going to burst. Our plane was late getting into O'Hare and they're holding the flight to Amsterdam for us. I wonder if any flight into or out of O'Hare is ever on time?

Terrible news at the boarding gate. They will not allow us to take our perfect little carry-on bags on board. We fumble through them frantically, getting out all we will need for the flight and then watch in fear and anger as they disappear into the bowels of O'Hare. Months of planning shot. Will we ever see our loved ones again—the perfectly planned and packed, albeit dun-colored, wardrobes for six weeks in Europe?

On the plane. Despite our excessive baggage worry, the flight over would be wonderful. A heavenly mixture of Dutch efficiency and chocolate. Would be wonderful except for the two idiots behind us. They have talked non-stop for hours. I want to rip their tongues from their heads. Both Phebe and I have begged them to please be quiet so that we can sleep. They will not. I am tempted to smother them with my tiny little airline pillow but it is so hard I am afraid I would just break their noses and they could continue to talk. It also has occurred to me to tell them I have a brain tumor which can only be helped by complete silence but I am so Irish superstitious that I am afraid I will develop one if I lie. So I decide to Offer It Up for a trip free of illness and accident, a peaceful and happy trip. Sometimes it pays to have been raised by nuns.

PHEBE
(ON THE PLANE)

I hear the voice of a man sitting behind me: "Was stationed in Germany 26 years ago. Haven't been back since. Plan to visit a family I knew there. I haven't told them I'm coming but I'm sure they'll be glad to see me..." Guess I'll write down everything he says to make me forget the hideous fact that soon we'll be taking off into thin air.

But here are the attendants. I must pay attention to them. I know most people are blasé about their instructions, but not me. "In the unlikely event we lose air pressure..." They're not fooling me with that "unlikely." I could create a worst case scenario in a minute (or as we Norwegians say, "et oyblik—an eyeblink"). Guess instead I'll try an affirmation: "God loves and protects me" might be good. But isn't it rather arrogant to expect Him to protect me above all others in the event of a crash over the Atlantic?

Why did I write "over the Atlantic"? I don't want to think about those cold, turbulent waters. Forget about air pressure and oxygen masks. Why don't the airline attendants give us training in lifeboat inflation and survival at sea? Not to worry. Dinner is on the way. I've always believed God would not let me die while I was eating,

Ex-soldier is holding forth again. He describes to his seatmate how he's been troubled lately with profuse nose-bleeds which cause blood clots to form in his throat. She replies in an unusually stentorian voice that he should perhaps try to relax, sit back, and not talk so much. Then she begins to talk on and on, tells him she's a French and Latin professor and her husband's a psychologist. "But I hate status," she says after firmly establishing hers. "My husband does, too. When he's on a plane, he never says 'Give me that seat because I'm a doctor.'" She goes on to tell a story about her granddaughter, who already knows how to read at age three. She learned to sound out words from the Dr. Seuss books and she can read every one of them. God forgive me for telling Caitlin stories. A sure way to get people to hate your grandchild.

However, the Ex-soldier has shut up about his blood clots and his worries that they'll choke him to death while he's asleep. But there's a new and more worrisome development. The shopping cart has arrived and Loud-voiced Woman has gone to patronize it. So Ex-soldier has leaned over and begun talking to Joan. She has made the mistake of answering him. He tells her the whole story over again of the blood clots and nosebleeds, then asks her what she plans to do when she lands in Amsterdam. He says he's alone and doesn't quite know what he'll do because he doesn't have a hotel reservation.

Why is Joan actually talking to him? Just a short while ago she whispered to me she would stuff their little airline pillows down both their throats if they didn't stop talking. Now she's acting as if she's his best friend. Next thing I know she'll be offering to share our hotel room with him.

Loud-voiced Woman has returned from her shopping foray just in time to hear Ex-soldier continue his whining. She tells him to shut off the light and go to sleep. "No, I need to read myself to sleep." "Reading will only over-stimulate you. Shut off the light and go to sleep." "I can't get comfortable. If I lie flat the blood clots will more likely choke me." "Do you feel the clots now?" "No, but they might form if I fall asleep."

The talking has stopped. Is it possible they've both fallen asleep? Oh, blessed silence. Joan is writing in her journal like a madwoman. I covet her book because it's got graph-lined paper of many colors. "One for each city," she announced smugly. It's also got tab indexes so she can label each one. Why didn't I buy one just like it? My plan was to wait and buy a small perfect journal in each new city. With my luck I'll spend endless hours searching and never finding. What made me think I'd want to waste even a moment on this trip looking for a suitable journal to write in?

It's dark in here now. All voices have quieted down. Turns out I found them comforting. Now the old question surfaces again: "What's normal air turbulence and what's abnormal?" We've had smooth sailing so far, but now we're hitting an occasional air pocket. No big deal. Maybe I need to repeat that. No big deal, no big deal, no big deal.

Joan's asleep. Loud-voiced Woman's asleep. Nose-bleeding Ex-soldier's asleep. All I can hear is the slap of someone's cards. The person seems to be endlessly shuffling them but never laying them out. There's hell for you. On an airplane in turbulence over the Atlantic Ocean with only one other person awake, someone who eternally shuffles cards for a Solitaire hand he never plays.

3. FACES IN THE WATER
Looking for Vincent and Anne in Amsterdam

MAY 9

JOAN

O n the Herengracht Canal: After a long flight, this is our day of
walking under water. And this is the city to do it in, with water
everywhere... in the canals that ring the city in serpentine ways and
in the cold, gray Atlantic that I feel is too close, held back just by
those tiny, man-made dikes.

Everyone told us to keep going as best we could this first day,
in spite of the jet lag, and that this activity would help us adjust
faster to the European time. I hope they're right as we're really
pushing ourselves and the strain is showing. Phebe, for one of
the few times since I've known her, was sarcastic and recalcitrant.
She knew that I was right and that it was going to rain but kept
refusing to take her umbrella. She finally did, and as soon as we
walked out of the hotel it started to pour. Of course she wouldn't
admit I was right, kept calling the downpour a "slight mist." I
was just as crabby and was kept from poking her severely with my

umbrella only by the knowledge that we had many more days to go together.

People on the outside don't understand. They see the bickering and competition and miss the truth that our friendship is also constant and loving. I often remind Phebe that perhaps God has sent me to her as a surrogate for her sister JoAnne who was my age exactly and who died when she was fourteen and Phebe was nineteen. Notice the similarity in the names, I tell her. This is probably a sign that you should be really nice to me and always do what I say.

At the airport we stumbled through the usual arrival mess and then took a train into town. Next to the train station was the VVV (the Dutch symbols for Tourist Bureau) where we went to get money changed and maps of the city. The woman behind the wicket said to Phebe, "Mind your money, Missy." I looked down and saw that both Phebe's purse and her wallet were wide open with dollars absolutely spilling out. This was a humiliating start for us, two women who have spent a fortune on hidden wallets.

Our hotel is absolutely wonderful. It's actually three 16th century houses cleverly joined together by a series of alpine-steep staircases and charming little hallways. It's right smack dab on the Herengracht Canal, one of the four major canals that ring the old city. All of the buildings on the Canal are ancient and all are a bit crooked. They were built on 15-foot log pilings, we were told, which are slipping at the rate of an inch or two a year.

Our room is tiny and in the back of the hotel but the view is so old-world it gives me the shivers. We look out on Dutch gable tops and chimney pots with flowers almost everywhere. And we have our very own little tiny bathroom with our first European bidet. Ah, so cosmopolitan we are, we are.

PHEBE

I was so excited to be at our first destination, that when we stepped up to the tourist desk, I didn't notice my purse had come unclasped. Joan warned me to be careful. I reassured her. "Most of my money is hidden away in the money belt around my waist safely tucked under my blouse and skirt."

She wondered how I was going to extricate it when the need arose. "You'll practically have to undress to get at it."

Our room is charming, spacious and immaculate. Floor to ceiling windows dressed with floral-printed drapes of heavy cotton. Twin beds merged under the same cream-painted headboard decorated with tiny delicate hand-painted flowers. The most delectable tub—deep enough for a full-fleshed person like myself to submerge completely. After bathing, we washed our plane clothes. Joan hung hers on the stretchable clothesline across the windows and I said, "Please. Does my first glimpse of Amsterdam have to be through your bras and panty hose?" She pointed out that was preferable to the way she'd smell tomorrow if she didn't do her wash. "And besides," she added. " what's so wonderful about the way you've draped yours over the chairs and luggage stand. Makes the room look messy."

Seems to me Joan is terribly cranky and a bit preoccupied. Jet lag perhaps. A few minutes ago she went down to the lobby to call Bob and returned in a fury because the long distance operator told her that her credit card had too many numbers. "What does that mean—too many numbers? Am I supposed to leave out some just to satisfy her desire for fewer numbers?" She continues fuming.

I'm torn between being glad I don't have to call a husband to let him know I've arrived safely and feeling sad because John doesn't care anymore. And I find myself being critical of how easily Joan gets angry. I have this image of myself as mild-mannered and calm and accepting of whatever happens. But the truth is I am capable of losing my temper, too. I remember well the time John so enraged me I threw a cup of coffee at him—well, not exactly at him but toward him. To my horror I realized, as I watched the cup arc into the air, that it was a much-beloved mug made for me by my potter friend. It even had my name on the side.

John's reaction? He very quietly got a broom, swept up all the pieces, mopped up the spilled coffee, then turned to me and asked in a maddeningly calm voice, "There now. Did that make you feel better?"

JOAN

After cleaning up and transferring our guilders to hidden wallets and remaining dollars to other hidden wallets, we set out to walk about the town. That soon exhausted what little energy we had left so we took a boat ride that went up and down the canals and then out into the harbor. There are houseboats everywhere, all gaily painted and full of flowers. That wouldn't be a bad way to live. Doesn't seem to make any difference what new place I'm in, I always think it would be fun to live there. Hope this means I'm daring and adventuresome, rather than just shallow, which I fear. After the canal ride, we went on walking doggedly until it was time for dinner.

Tonight we went to a Rijsstafels or Rice Table, which Amsterdam is famous for, because of all their colonial days in Indonesia. The food was wonderfully interesting—15 small dishes on a hot tray. And mysterious. I couldn't tell what kind of meat was in anything. I ate it all in spite of the fact that I worried that some of the dishes might have, as an ingredient, someone's former domestic pet.

PHEBE

We've decided to plunge right into Amsterdam by taking a canal boat tour. I plunged in a little too fast for Joan. She wanted to take another boat because this one was too crowded but I downright refused to wait. Just plowed ahead and got on the boat so she was forced to follow me. She had no choice, unless she wanted to lose me our first day abroad. Sometimes I surprise myself by my assertiveness, or would some call it stubbornness?

Our guide tells us we're on the only natural river in Amsterdam, the Amstel.

The canals were all hand-dug in the 17th century and have sixteen locks to flush out the canal water daily. Oh, those Dutch and their wholesome ways, except for their liberal attitude toward drugs and prostitutes.

We've passed the first Protestant church built after the Reformation (1614), then an enormous pagoda-like floating

Chinese restaurant that seats 900 and an industrial park which features a monstrously ugly Shell Oil building with coral "windows" painted on brown cement and an odd surreal abstract sculpture on top. "Makes me ashamed to be an American," I tell Joan. "Why?" she asks. "Shell Oil is Dutch, you know." I don't believe her, but I decide not to argue with her.

Here's a Lutheran church with a swan at the very top, and the guide tells us the swan is the symbol of Lutheranism, something I've never heard before. Maybe that's why I'm so drawn to swan figurines and vases and soaps and candy dishes. For a while, swans were threatening to overwhelm my decor. Then Joan said I should do something about the swans. This was when she was under the influence of a tyrannical decorator who persuaded her to give up her entire lion collection.

We've passed many houseboats and our guide tells us there are over 3000 in the canals, including a wooden one called the Cat-Boat. The 80-year-old owner takes care of the stray cats of Amsterdam. Sometimes she has over eighty cats in residence. The guide tells us when houseboats are registered, they have running water and electricity. Sotto voce, Joan says, "So what happens if they're not registered? Do they have to dip their water out of the canal and read by candlelight?"

Now we're passing a bridge the guide tells us has a prison built onto it. Sure enough, there's a man I take to be a prisoner looking out the window at us. I want to wave, but think better of it. I wouldn't want him to think he's a regular citizen, instead of one who needs the punishment of being ignored by an American tourist.

We come to the narrowest canal, Berlingscost, where the houses jut right into the canal and then to the Golden Bent where the largest and richest houses are, many of which have been turned into banks and consulates. When we pass a statue of St. Michael slaying the dragon, I look up from my writing to ask Joan, my expert on saints, what she knows about him. She seems rather bemused. I have to ask her twice. Then she says she's glad I've decided to talk to her again: "You were writing so constantly you hardly had time to really look at the sights." I said how it might be a good idea for her to write more, too. She's been bemoaning the fact that she'll have no career to go back to since she quit the agency before we left. I keep reminding her that she *does* have a career—she's a writer with a half-finished novel which her creative writing professor at the U told her was publishable. Writing in her journal will keep her juices flowing until she gets back to her precious Mac again, I tell her, sounding rather like a teacher. Then I bend down once more to write my last entry about the canal trip, that we've come full circle back to the Amstel River and to a skinny 17th century hand-operated bridge. The guide points out a houseboat owned by an American artist who claims to be Victor IV. He's made a sign pointing to a swan's nest on his boat. "Swan's Nest, three (3) eggs."

After we got off the canal boat, we walked down Kalver Straat to a wonderful church, Franciscus Xaverius Kristberg. Inside Joan bought a candle to light and so did I. When in a Catholic church, do as the Catholics do. In front of a statue of the Virgin I prayed for Erik and Mary and Caitlin and Rolf and Leah, suddenly missing them very much. I love the Catholics for their veneration of Mary. I like to believe that Jesus learned his theology from her—messages of turn the other cheek, love your enemies, pray for them who spitefully use you.

I wanted to linger in that church, but we needed to press on to our evening meal. We found a wonderful Indonesian place where we had our first meal on European soil— Rijsttafels or Rice Table, consisting of boiled rice, beef in a spicy red sauce, beef in a spicy yellow sauce, beef in a spicy soy sauce, chicken in a spicy yellow sauce, barbecued pork with peanut sauce on a stick, vegetables in coconut milk, steamed bean sprouts, half an egg in Balinese sauce, Javanese meatballs, dessicated coconut with peanuts, fried and spicy soy bean cake, Indonesian pickles, Indonesian fruit salad, fried bananas, shrimp chips—all for about nine dollars and seven cents. Why did I say "about" when I figured it out to the penny.

JOAN

First bedtime in Europe: Phebe and I are both so tired and crabby tonight. We know enough to settle into our books and journal writing without much talking. I think one true test of how good friends you are with someone is how comfortable you are with silences.

We've been really angry with each other only once in our long friendship. That was the year I gave Leah one of Delilah's kittens for her birthday. I had tried so hard to find homes for all those kittens. I had one left and I was desperate. I put the kitten in a basket and tied a big bow on it. Leah was thrilled. Phebe was really mad.

And Phebe and that cat never did get along. She had to keep a broom outside her bedroom door for years because the cat would attack her feet when she came out in the morning. That was the first of many funny felines for Phebe. The worst was George, a huge, battered old tomcat with so many scars and scabs and puckered eyelids, he scared people. He also had an enormous open sore on his neck that never would heal. George had the strangest habit. He would lie in wait outside a neighbor's back door and when they chanced to open it, George would streak in and head for the basement where he would leap up on their furnace and defy anyone to remove him. The neighbors were terrified and Phebe or John would be called to come over with a broom to get George out. This went on for years and there wasn't much neighborly feeling left between the two families after while.

PHEBE

Back in our hotel room, my old malaise—anxiety, apprehension and unutterable sadness—has temporarily struck again. I say "temporarily" because I know it always lifts, but right now I feel so alone. Perhaps it's because Joan seems withdrawn, missing Bob and angry because she can't reach him. I don't want to be an old maid, the word used when I was a child to refer to those unlucky souls whom no man had chosen. I think I still want a mate, messy as that might make my life. The last time I was overseas, I was 22 and searching for romance. I thought maybe I'd find my true love in Norway. Maybe that's where I was destined to live and raise my family, a sort of reverse immigrant. I actually believed, in those days, I was only half a person until I was united with another. Maybe my other half was in the country of my father's birth.

On this trip, I'm not looking for romance. The idea that any man could be attracted to me at my age and in my shape seems ludicrous. Would I even want a romantic encounter? Do I truly want a mate again? When I was married, did I strive for ever-greater intimacy? Certainly not during the last years of our marriage when a pall hung over our relationship. Nothing I did seemed right in John's eyes. But to be fair, I don't think I accepted him as he was, either. I kept trying to change him. Strange how all the unresolved fragments of my marriage surface to haunt me on this trip. We've been separated three years, but I still find myself writing about him, wondering what went wrong, how the marriage might have been redeemed.

MAY 10

JOAN

If this first Dutch breakfast is any indication of what we're going to find in Europe, we're going to have to do a powerful lot of walking to keep from fleshing out nicely. This morning we had pots of good, hot coffee, three kinds of cheese, ham, four kinds of bread, butter, two kinds of jam and a hot, hard-cooked egg.

The flowers here—mein gott! Glorious. The bouquets in the salon are so huge and elaborate I knew they must be preparing for a wedding but the nice girl at the desk just laughed and said, "No, they're for everyday." Every table in the dining room has its own incredible bouquet too. For one insane moment I consider asking where I could get some bulbs to take home. And then I remember. I don't grow things. I destroy them with my killer brown thumbs. All I have to do is walk through nurseries and little seedlings shiver and curl up from fright. I don't understand it. I spring from a mother who could plant Popsicle sticks and get peonies.

Her garden was a triumph where she worked hard all summer. Besides planting and picking, Mom was at war with birds who ate her raspberries. Her coverings became more and more elaborate until one entire section of the garden was covered in tulle-like netting. Still the birds won. "I don't know, Murph," Mom said. "I think those birds have had commando training. I'm convinced the little feathered devils are crawling up under the netting."

PHEBE

First thing we did after we got up was make our list of things to see in Amsterdam: Anne Frank's house; Begijnhof, a pensioner's residence; Riksmuseum; Van Gogh Museum. Then we went to breakfast in the hotel restaurant where out the window we could see graffiti on the canal wall. We overheard a husband and wife with two small children discussing the canal graffiti:

Husband: That graffiti is illegal. I hate to see walls and buildings disfigured.

Wife: It's the mark of a free society.

Husband: But it's so undisciplined.

Wife: People have the right to express themselves.

Husband: I think it's ugly. And all these children who walk around with spiky hair and disgusting clothes, they're ugly too.

Wife: But it's their right to do that.

Husband: Graffiti is still illegal. You're going to argue for their right to deface public property?

Wife: I argue for their right to express themselves.

Husband: But we need rules. We need discipline. This sort of thing you'd think would be more common in societies where other means of expression are suppressed.

Wife: Like the famous billboards of China? Or Poland? Sarah, what ARE you putting on your bread, sweetheart? Emma, why are you picking your bread apart? And that's ENOUGH jelly!

I listen to their conversation and feel a yearning for the days when I was young and our kids were little. A golden aura surrounds those years. I can see us so clearly, sitting around the oak dining room table, morning sunlight streaming in on our faces. Leah's in her high chair, mucking about in her oatmeal. I leave for a few minutes to get some brown sugar in the kitchen. When I come back, Rolf, who's three and very jealous of this interloper sister, is pressing his finger into her forehead with just a tad too much force. "Do you know what's going to happen to you?" She gazes at him with her sweet hazel eyes, suspecting nothing. "You're going to GROW!"

And they did grow, far too fast. I grew too, went back to teaching high school English, found I loved it more than I had before I was married. Then I discovered poetry and my desire to write. Somehow I didn't have enough time to do it all. Why didn't I pay more attention to what was happening between me and John? Why didn't I understand how important it was to keep the family together? Why did I take John for granted, assuming he'd always be there no matter how I neglected him? Why do I blame myself for everything that went wrong?

JOAN

At Anne Frank's House: People come pounding up the stairs, laughing and talking loudly until they reach the first level. They come through the office and start up the secret stairs behind the bookcases. Then the quiet starts and spreads, it is as silent as a tomb upstairs where Anne lived. The horror is that it is so ordinary. She was just like me. I can tell from the things she saved, from her bulletin board that we would have liked each other, would have been friends and now she isn't here, isn't anywhere. The horror is that I feel if I start to cry I will never be able to stop.

PHEBE

Here I am in Anne Frank's house, where I've just read a description of the infamous Kristallnacht of November 1938.

That was the year after my mother died and I was sent to live with my grandparents in Duluth. My grandmother spoke little English—she'd been in her 30's when she came from Sweden—and I worried constantly because I couldn't understand her. She had wild mood swings, scolding and shaming me one moment and smothering me with sloppy kisses the next.

Mrs. Goldberg, the mother of my friend Harold, took me, the motherless child, under her wing, cosseting me and feeding me strange and wonderful food, like Hamantoshen, that delicious

Purim cookie filled with dates and nuts. Many an evening I sat in the Goldberg living room, part of their family, playing Chinese checkers with Harold. How safe we all were there in America while such unspeakable things were happening in Germany.

Anne's bulletin board called to me after I'd looked at the famous little plaid diary with a lock and a key. She had tacked up pictures of American movie stars—Deanna Durbin, Norma Shearer, Ginger Rogers. Under the famous photo of herself, she had written: "This is a photo as I wish myself to look all the time. Then maybe I would have a chance to come to Hollywood." A little girl hiding from the Nazis in Amsterdam dreamed of one day becoming a movie star. When I was her age, I was writing in a diary, too, the little Five Year Diary my best friend, Janice Lindberg, gave me my first Christmas in Duluth. While I was writing about playing Chinese checkers with Harold Goldberg, the Nazis were preparing the great extinction that would take Anne's life.

JOAN

Sitting in the garden of The Begijnhof: This translates roughly as Beguine Court and it's a 16th Century, perfectly-preserved square of homes built by the wealthy for old-age pensioners of the 1500's and still used today for the same purpose. A writer in one of my tour books calls it the most enchanting spot in Europe and I can see why, sitting here on a comfortable, middle-aged sort of bench, looking quietly around me. The flowers are blooming madly in the yards and windows of every house and in the little park in the middle of the square. All the windows in the charming old houses are covered with dazzling white lace curtains. Several also feature old ladies peeking out to see who's here. Instead of being embarrassed at being caught peeking, they seem to know they're the very nicest part of the Begijnhof and wave gaily at you when you spot them.

Why does it always seem to be old ladies, left alone and lonely? It starts when we put our child on a bus for kindergarten. It's no wonder we cry. We're crying for our lost babies and we're crying because we know our lonely years have started. When the babies come home, they're different. You can see it in their eyes. They've moved on, left us behind. From now on, every year, they'll tell us a little less, need other people a little more.

But children have to leave, we want them to. If we've done our job right, they'll leave without guilt, only looking back when they want to, not because they need us too much or worry that we need them. Oh, what sad thoughts. Must be because I'm a little tired from the trip. And I'm depressed about not having a job anymore. I've joked for years about not having any feminine talents, cooking, sewing, decorating. What will I do when I get home? I've given up my career. All I have to look forward to is retirement. And years to go before I can collect Social Security. Maybe I should move over here and make my home with these sweet ladies. It's so lovely and peaceful here, I'm sure I could figure out the next step.

Instead, I was almost asleep in a minute, breathing in the soft smells of rainy soil and spring blooms, when a church bell rang the Angelus. What a surprise. Diagonally across, through the little central garden, is a Catholic Church. Well, when God makes it this easy to visit Him, how can I refuse? I wandered into church and lit some candles for my dead, asked for some light on what I should do next with my life and a pardon for the sins that are resting on my soul.

PHEBE

After a full day, we walked two canals over from our hotel and looked for the famous "tourist menu" signs Arthur Frommer writes of, but didn't find them. Wearied and knee-sore, we finally settled for an ordinary-looking restaurant where we ended up having an inexpensive and delicious meal. I ordered plaice, a fish Joan says is very common in England, the stuff of fish and chips. So far, we've found only excellent food in Amsterdam.

On the way home we saw two red lights above stores. We've had several fights about whether or not to visit Amsterdam's famed red light district. I thought maybe the sighting of those lights would satisfy her desire to wander about in a neighborhood where prostitutes ply their trade. But she said she couldn't believe I wanted to deprive myself of such an interesting experience. "I suppose I should take a more liberal view of prostitution," I said. "After all, some have said that marriage is legalized prostitution, only it doesn't pay as well. I've never held to such a cynical view myself." Then she surprised me by saying there might be some truth in that, adding I was much better off not married. "I've never seen you happier than since you left John. The single life seems to suit you perfectly." That didn't sound like Joan, the defender of the sanctity of marriage, who goes into a fit if she can't talk to her husband every day.

In the end, I still refused to go into the red light district, but told her she was free to go by herself, that I'd stay alone in the hotel. She wasn't about to venture into that part of town without me, so my refusal kept her from doing what she wanted.

Of course, I couldn't just let the subject drop. I had to continue with my justification for not wanting to see what Joan termed one of the famous "tourist attractions" of the city. "I don't consider the red light district a tourist attraction. Since I've been teaching at MCAD, art is my life. Museums and galleries and famous buildings—those are the tourist attractions I want to see." She wouldn't let me get by with that pretentious pronouncement and launched into a little tirade about how I didn't fool her with my so-called new-found interest in art. She knew what my *real* interests were and they weren't any more high brow nor intellectual than hers. I said my back and knees hurt and I didn't want to talk about it anymore.

It's true, my back and knees do hurt dreadfully. They've been bothering me since I got here, but I've been determined to walk through the pain. We're in EUROPE and we want to "get the good out of" every minute, as Joan's mother would say. We rest as often as possible, though, and are grateful for every bench sighting. I'm especially hoping to see benches in museums because I want to write about the paintings and sculptures and it's hard to write standing up.

MAY 11
JOAN

Rijksmuseum: The Rembrandts are incredible. And, of course, there are so many of them. My favorite is his "Self Portrait." It's so loving in spite of the fact that he shows every skin flaw, every pit, every line. Still, looking at it, you just know that Rembrandt thought he was a nice old man, peaceful and kind. His eyes are soft and guileless, you feel you'd like to meet him, would trust him to paint your portrait fairly, without coldness or meanness. It reminds me of my dad, so recently dead, so much on my mind on this trip. It isn't that Rembrandt looks anything like my father, it's just that incredible kindness that some old people have in their faces. My mother used to say that if you live to be seventy, you finally have the face you deserve, the one you've earned. At ninety-three, when he died, my father looked like a sweet saint.

Rembrandt's "Jewish Bride" makes me homesick for Bob so I bought a reproduction on a postcard to mail him. It shows the bridegroom with his hand on the breast of the blushing, not complaining, bride. I sent Bob Card #6 last night and will mail this one today. Phebe has been making a lot of fun of me lately about the postcards, but she'll be sorry when the trip is nearly over and she has to spend all of one of her last days writing postcard after postcard. "Does the story of the tortoise and the hare bring anything to mind, postcard-wise?" I asked her.

There's a roomful or more of Steens and they are a surprise to me. I hadn't known about him. His paintings are funny. Steen was a rabid teetotaler, horribly against alcohol. Many of his paintings show the folly and waste of drinking, the poor influence it has on the children of the families in the pictures. I bought a copy of "Family Scene" for my friend's office, showing a drunken family, broken eggs and crockery on the floor, crying children. That should put some fear into her recovering alcoholic patients.

There's another whole room smash full of Franz Hals' paintings. Every one, my guidebook says, is a "triumph of the artist as psychologist/priest." I'm not positive I know what they mean by that except that Hals does seem to see things in the people he paints that they'd rather he didn't. For instance, in Hals' "Marriage Portrait," the groom, Isaac Massa, looks smug and stupid, his bride, Beatrix van der Laen, sly and greedy. Wonder if Hals got paid for that painting.

But my absolute favorites here are the Vermeers. They are filled with such light, a beautiful, clear, mystical, white light. And every painting is a puzzle of some sort to me. Who is wrestling on the ground in that painting? What is the news in the letter that Blue Lady is reading? How did the woman in the next painting keep her floor of black and white tiles so shining, so gleaming? I had a floor exactly like that on Lake of the Isles and if the black tiles had enough wax to gleam, the white tiles turned yellow. What a stupid thing to be thinking about in one of the greatest museums in the world. But I really would like to know how she did it, even though I know Vermeer deserves better from me. I'd like to be able to tell him, "Jan, you're a genius. These are the paintings I could walk right into. I know I would be happy in your light, that incredible light."

PHEBE

Here we are at the Rijksmuseum and I'm overwhelmed, not quite sure how even to begin writing about all this magnificence. Now I'm embarrassed about saying to Joan, "Art is my life." She's over there in front of a Rembrandt, writing copiously as if she were a seasoned art critic. So what's holding me up? All these years I've been teaching at MCAD I've always urged my students to just plunge in, not worry about what they say, at least not in their journals. Time to follow my own advice.

Here's "Venus and Adonis" by Ferdinand Bol (1616-1680), an artist I've never heard of, but good enough to end up in this museum. Venus is mostly naked, swathed in white drapery over her lower torso. Adonis is wearing a cute little red garment, while Cupid is totally naked. I am reminded of those early Shirley Temple videos. In her autobiography she told how her directors made her appear in parodies of adult movies when she was three years old. She portrayed sexy vamps, dressed only in a drooping diaper. Why have I been reminded of this as I stand here in the Riksmuseum? Better move on to the Rembrandts.

Rembrandt's "Jeremiah Lamenting the Destruction of Jerusalem" reminds me of the soloist in one of my father's churches. At this rate. it's going to take me awhile to get through this museum. Mr. Afton's voice was past its prime, but once a year he convinced my father to let him sing

"The Holy City." I loved his wild histrionic gestures and exaggerated mannerisms, like a small town Pavarotti. Oh, how he lamented the destruction of Jeruselem. Then without warning, his aging voice would crack or quaver and the spell would be broken.

My dad sometimes sang solos in church, too, but only when no one else was available. My father's voice was the opposite of Mr. Afton's, a basso profundo that seemed to come from deep within his stomach. His favorite song was "I'm a Pilgrim and I'm a stranger and I can tarry, I can tarry but a while," words which carried out his favorite theme that our life in this "vale of sorrow and tears" was ephemeral, but that the new Jerusalem awaited us. Earth was but a way station. Our real home was elsewhere "our treasures were laid up, somewhere beyond the blue."

JOAN

Van Gogh Museum: A huge, modern building full of nothing but Vincent Van Gogh paintings and drawings. It's really just a branch of the Rijksmuseum and an easy walk away, about two blocks. Here are the originals of the prints we all had on our walls as young marrieds—the orchards at Arles, the sunflowers, Vincent's blue room, and his self portrait. But these are the real things, the honest-to-gosh Van Goghs.

I learned something new about Van Gogh today. His father was a minister and he had studied for the ministry too. I wonder if a conflict between his raging creativity and his strict belief system helped to drive him mad.

Right before Van Gogh died, he started laying on paint thickly, so that in some places it looked almost as though he were trying to get rid of it. The paint sticks out from a 1/2-inch to an inch from most of these last canvases. It's easy to see this because you can get incredibly close to the paintings. There's only a very narrow white line about a foot out from the wall beyond which we aren't supposed to go. Getting this close to them, they fair take the breath out of you with their lavishness.

I remember that after my friend Merry killed herself, they found bags and bags and bags of brand new clothes in her drawers and closets. Five or six swim suits, never worn. Twenty pairs of panty hose. Sweaters with the price tags still attached. Cosmetics in profusion, purses in every color of the rainbow. She was a woman who never spent money on herself unless forced to. And yet she must have spent so many of her last hours shopping, buying, bringing things home she would never use. Someone told me that this sad lavishness happens often just before a suicide. It seems to be a clinging to life, this consuming and waste. Perhaps it was death that Van Gogh was trying to hold away with his thick paint.

After the funeral, Merry's sister asked me if I didn't want some of these never-worn clothes, never-opened cosmetics. But I couldn't bear to have them near me. They seemed to me to be Merry's last hope and I couldn't, wouldn't wear her failure.

PHEBE

We've moved on to the Van Gogh Museum. Soon I'll be looking at the real thing instead of the posters I've known for years. When John and I moved into our attic apartment in 1953, we hung a poster of "Starry Night" above our bed. We needed a spotlight to illuminate it because that room had no natural light. It was really just a large closet which the landlord hoped we'd believe was a bedroom. In the living room, "Sunflowers" to go with the bright yellow drapes I made on the Singer sewing machine. John carved a woodblock design, then hand-printed it on the endless yards of sailcloth. I can still see him patiently inking the stamp, laying it carefully on the material, then standing on the block to make sure the brown ink imprint was firm and true. The design was the symbol for infinity to remind us of our love, which would of course last forever.

Van Gogh was a preacher's son who grew up in a gloomy household and knew death at an early age, as I did. His mother lost a baby a year before Vincent was born. She was still grieving when she became pregnant with Vincent and named him the same as the one who'd died. Every day Vincent walked through the cemetery next to his father's church and saw his own name on the headstone.

Van Gogh followed in his father's footsteps and became a minister, one with a strong social conscience. He took a lowly parish so he could work with peasants.

Many of his paintings give us an intimate look at their lives. In "The Evening," where a couple in their humble room are illuminated by glowing candlelight, the woman is bent over her sewing, the man over his woodcarving. Baby's asleep in a little basket and a small cat lounges nearby. We feel tenderness and compassion toward these hard-working folks who live so simply, yet seem contented. Hard to see in such lovely evocations of everyday life, the man who later suffered such agonizing bouts of what may have been schizophrenia. I am reminded of what my father used to say when I asked him why he didn't vote for candidates who'd work for social reform and more programs for the poor. "The poor you have always with you, Phebe." When I'd protest that was a cop out, he'd add, "It's in the Bible," as if that would clinch it for me.

I could stay here forever, meditating on these paintings. Why move on to any other painters? Especially when I'm not sure I'll ever see them again in this life. Why did I write "in this life"? Do I have some vision of a hereafter which would give me an eternity to look at all the art, listen to all the music and read all the books? Borges once said he believed heaven would be a giant library. I hope he's right.

Back at our hotel, we were excited to see an Ingmar Bergman film was on TV and settled back to enjoy it, then realized it was in Swedish with Dutch subtitles, two languages even Joan's nuns weren't able to teach her.

MAY 12

JOAN

I woke up this morning too early. At 4:30am, everything is gray to the bottom of my soul. What seemed like a free and courageous act, quitting the agency, now seems rankest stupidity. I simply handed over to Bob everything I worked to build up in the past twenty years. And I haven't got a clue of what I want to do next. I started thinking this morning that if Bob decides he's in love with someone new while I'm in Europe, I would have to get a job quickly, maybe one in a travel agency. Then I realized that I'm not qualified. I have no knowledge of computers, which is a must. Also, I'm pretty old to be looking for, not just a new job, but a whole new career. Who will hire me? I have plenty of office clothes. Maybe I could be a hostess in a restaurant. Go back to my first real job, long distance telephone operator. That's probably a job that's been computerized now too.

I'm also nervous about traveling to Brussels today. I don't think my high school French is up to the job. Why didn't I pay more attention to Sister Louis Phillippe? My reading and writing were okay but when we had French Conversation and it was my turn to talk, Sister would turn towards the blackboard and I could see her shoulders shaking with laughter. Thirty-five years ago!

Last night we watched television. *Blazing Saddles* and *Murder She Wrote*, both in English, of course, and both with Dutch subtitles at the bottom of the screen. Wouldn't this be a keen way to learn languages? Perhaps this is why practically everyone you meet here speaks some English. There were also programs in French and German. I would have a hard time learning Dutch. It's a very difficult language, sounds German but even more gutteral.

Finally Phebe woke up and we packed up and went down for our enormous Dutch breakfast. Didn't leave a crumb, of course. I'm a Product of the Great Depression. If I've paid for it, I'll eat it even if it makes me sick. As I was taking my last look out at the rooftops from our bedroom window I saw a stork! I'm just positive that's what it was with those long, long legs. The sighting of a stork is supposed to bring you lots of luck. Seems a good omen for the next leg of our trip. Already I hate to leave Amsterdam, feel at home here, which is really strange when I remember how foreign it seemed just days ago. It isn't at all like I thought it would be either. I got my ideas from childhood books like Hans Brinker that had frozen canals, windmills and Dutch housewives out scrubbing their stoops. Actually, Amsterdam is really dirty.

The other sad thing about Amsterdam is all the lost children. Drugs aren't illegal here and some are even free. The town seems full of young addicts waiting for their next fix. In the train station, I sat next to one who had a packet of white powder he was sniffing. He was so young, so pathetically dirty and thin with knobby, little-boy wrists hanging out of his shirt. As we walked down the train platform, we saw another filthy young man rolling a sleeping crippled boy, looking through his pockets and rucksack. The second boy never woke up, sleeping off his drug in the dirty, noisy station, with his crutches beside him.

4. WHEN IN BRUSSELS, ORDER MUSSELS

In the ultimate Renaissance Mall

MAY 12

PHEBE

On our way to Paris, passing from Leyden to Haarlem, we saw fields and fields of tulips, row upon row, flashing by on both sides of the train, dazzling our eyes. I thought of my friend, who grew up in Holland, telling how he and his family had to eat tulip bulbs during the Nazi occupation.

Now we're passing enormous piles of cut-off tulip heads. These tulips were grown for the bulbs, not for the splendor of the blossoms. They'll get their chance to bloom another day. A new start. That's what I want, a new start, a chance to bloom again as an unmarried woman, all regrets forgotten, all resentments released. Trust me to extract a little life lesson from a pile of tulip heads.

We arrived in Brussels without a hotel reservation, confident we'd find the perfect place. Surely our budget guidebook would come through for us. After we found one that looked good, we consulted our maps, then argued crossly about which direction to go. Joan hated to admit it, but I had pinpointed the location exactly. Soon we found our darling little hotel. When we were safely in our room, our bags unpacked, our ablutions performed, we took off in search of food. We decided to eat a little paté to stave off starvation until we could find the elegant restaurant Joan's friend had recommended. There we'd unleash our full appetites.

Our hunger appeased, we wandered around the magnificent Grand Place where guild halls of various trades are located. The streets were quaint and narrow in this ancient quarter. Despite our decision not to waste time shopping on this trip, we stopped to buy large sheer cotton floral scarves. I know they'll come in handy when the wind tosses our hair on the streets of all the European cities we plan to visit.

JOAN

On the 9:28am train to Brussels: We're flying by fields and fields of flowers. It was a cold spring so we were lucky. Usually the blooming season is long over by now but we're deliciously right in the middle of it and it is glorious. Spring bursting forth in acres of color. A field of mauve, followed by scarlet, closely tailed by gold. And again and again. The earth here is flat and stretches as far as I can see, without a house or tree, just row on row, field on field of these flowers. I wonder if all this flat land has been reclaimed from the sea, held back by dikes and courage. Where once only kelp waved, now there are tulips and daffodils, anemones and pale narcissus.

The trip would be so wonderful except for our traveling companions in our plush, first class compartment. They are a young couple from Toronto. She is lovely and I would like to talk to her but he takes over the conversation for both of them, quelling her with a fearsome look when she ventures an opinion, or even a little sigh or laugh. He is so incredibly boring I can hardly believe it. His sole topic of conversation is how to get the most for your money in Europe, especially by cheating people. His "tips" for getting farther on a franc include not tipping people in restaurants at all. "After all, they'll never see you again, you're just passing through."

Another is how to ride buses in Rome all week for one ticket. "They never ask to see your ticket. If they do and you're caught, they give you a summons, you're supposed to go to court and pay a big fine. But you'll be long gone."

In the midst of all his bragging about how he cheated everyone he could in Europe, he kept telling us how dishonest everyone we were going to meet on the Continent would be. Horror story after horror story about how they were just waiting for plump, little, trusting middle-aged pigeons like us and how Europeans would soon part us from every travelers check and credit card in our possession. His sightseeing tips are equally stupid. "Ladies, I promise you can see Venice in less than a day."

I quit listening to him, physically turned away and filled my eyes with flowers. And brooded. I am very lonely this morning for my son. An aching loneliness. This is funny because I really don't see that much of him at home. I think it's because of all the wonderful things I've seen so far on this trip, all the ones to come. I want to share them with Dennis. I love him so much, I want him to have everything I have, including all these European experiences. He's so open to new ideas, new things, so accepting. I hope he always stays this way. How awful it would be to have a son like that fool sitting across from me this morning.

When the train arrived in Brussels, Phebe and I were in the midst of such an intense discussion of her refusal to visit the red light district in Amsterdam that we missed all the signs and walked the wrong way out of the Gare Central, making a huge circle and getting nowhere. Then it struck us funny to be so busy talking about Amsterdam, we were missing seeing Brussels. Well, we have to face the fact that we're not going to have the time, even going as slowly as we are, to see everything. We're both so passionately interested in everything over here that it's difficult to compromise and miss seeing anything. This is one of the things that's different about doing the trip at our age, instead of when we were in college. We know now that time can run out on us, that we can't do everything we wish, that we have to make choices.

On the way down to the Old Town from the station, we passed a beautiful church, very ancient. It was started in the 5th Century and was originally called St. Gudule. Then scholars at the Vatican in the 7th Century proved there was no such person as St. Gudule and ordered the pastor to change the name, which he did. It is now called St. Michael's, but everyone in Brussels still calls it St. Gudule. For 800 years, they've insisted on calling their church by its original name. Now that's stubborn.

Our hotel is right off the square, a 15th Century townhouse. Outside it seems to be the same as when it was built; inside it's completely redone, quite modern and so wonderful. Our room is charming, comfortable and the view out of our window is pure Middle Ages. Tonight we tried our first European light-the-hall-just-for-a-minute buttons. You press the first hall button as you get off the elevator. It's supposed to light the first section of hall until you arrive at the second button. This never works for us and we are always fumbling around in the pitch black for the next button. Europeans must be used to running like hell down hotel corridors with this kind of lighting system.

MAY 13

PHEBE

When I looked out the high casement window just a few minutes ago, I saw a man's socks and shoes set out to air on the window ledge. Reminded me of John and how he used to carefully place his running shoes and sweaty socks to air outside our bedroom window. "I wish you'd throw your socks down the clothes chute," I'd say, and John would answer, "Well, I can't do that because then I don't know when I might see them again." So why did I suddenly miss him when I saw those shoes?

After a delicious breakfast we walked to the Church of St. Nicholas, designed to be a merchant church, set deliberately in the midst of the market place. Where better for me, the consummate consumer, to settle than here? As I sit in this comfortable pew, my eye is drawn to a strange design above one of the side altars—an eye enclosed within a triangle with rays of light emanating from it and little cloud-like circles in each of the four corners. This design is above the grotto or niche that holds St. Nicholas' statue. Where have I seen this eye before? Joan reminds me that it's familiar because the same eye is on all our dollar bills. Guess I've never really looked at one before.

That eye also reminds me of what our father told us daily: the eye of Jesus is always upon you. Furthermore, my father believed Jesus was coming any day to take to Heaven all those who had been saved by His blood. I never believed I was one of the saved. I was always up to no good, always getting into trouble. It was as if being the minister's daughter were a mandate to be naughty. Playing cards, for instance, was strictly forbidden. I felt guilty even when I would go to my friend's house to play "Old Maid." At eight I was already guilt-ridden. No wonder I bargained with God the day my mother died: "Please, I promise to be good if you won't let her die."

Joan and I often argue about which is stronger—Lutheran or Catholic guilt. I always insist it's harder to be Lutheran. Catholics are less guilt-ridden because they have a beautiful system of confession and penance. Somehow the Lutheran church of my childhood didn't do as good a job of making me understand my sins were forgiven. I grew up feeling quite worthless. After all, God did let my mother die, despite my promises.

I'm reading a guide book of Joan's which points out that the origin of the Grand Place seems obvious from the street names—Rue des Harengs (Herring Street), Rue Chair et Pain (Meat and Bread Street) and Rue au Beurre (Butter Street). A farmers' market, but much grander than any back home.

And much older. Already in 1380 the Grand Place was in full swing. We also wandered past a whole group of statues of women—the Seven Virtues. Can't find any reference to them in my guide book. Not important enough to be included, I suppose. I find it fascinating that these virtues are embodied as women. I have to admit I've not been too interested in mythology or even in art history, for that matter, until this trip. Travel broadens my awareness of the vastness of my ignorance. The important thing to remember, however, is that I'll have plenty of incentive to find out new information when I get back. At least, that's the hope—that I'll read all the guide books I'm accumulating, re-read journal entries, and hie myself to the library where I'll be transformed into the scholar I've always yearned to be, but was always too undisciplined to achieve.

MAY 14
JOAN

Last night we decided to go out for a big splurge dinner to a famous, old, restaurant, highly recommended by a dear friend at home who lived here for several years. "And when in Brussels, " she said, "be sure to order mussels at this wonderful restaurant." Who could forget such a rhyming travel tip? And so off we went in search of mussels on our first night in Brussels. The restaurant was exactly as we had imagined a Belgian restaurant should be, old and cultured and lovely. The service was divine and so were the people. Next to us was a beautifully-dressed couple and their tiny dog who sat right next to me on the banquette, following each morsel of food I raised to my lips with large, liquid brown eyes.

The most embarrassing thing happened to me there. I walked right in on a man urinating. It was also awfully funny because I thought the little old lady guarding the bathroom was going to faint. She did everything she could, short of tackling me and sitting on my head, to keep me from walking the wrong way and getting into the men's room. Well, actually not a room, just part of a room. This was the funniest W.C. I've ever seen, just one big room with no partitions or dividers except for a large table in the center of the room. If you chanced to walk or look left, you were in the men's room. Turn right and you were in the woman's side with the nervous little femme d'chambre.

This was the fault of that dolt on the train. Although I didn't really believe him, he got me so nervous about crime in Europe that I had stuffed my enormous travel billfold into the top of my pantyhose with the cord cutting cruelly into my waist. Until I met him, I had kept my money and passport completely safe and hidden beneath my left arm.

Well, it was time to pay the bill and I had neglected to remove any money. The extricating of the billfold was made doubly painful by the openness of the bathroom. I was sure that a horde of Belgian men would walk in on me and wonder just what in God's name was bulging out of my pantyhose. And perhaps one would be the same man I had surprised urinating.

This actually seemed right for Brussels, a city whose most famous tourist attraction is the Mannikin Pis, a statue and fountain devoted to the art of male urination. We walked and walked to get to the Mannikin Pis and when we got there it was this tiny statue, a little boy going to the bathroom, completely surrounded by tourists watching him go. As they have watched him for generations.

My mother mentions this statue in her European journal. Just barely. I think she was puzzled that it should be considered a tourist "must," as I am. But she doesn't say that. Of course, she was very good at ignoring things she considered to be in poor taste. I can never remember her telling an off-color joke. Once when my uncle did at a holiday table, she simply stared at him and then changed the subject. It was devastating.

If I had been in that situation, I would probably have blurted out something insulting, the whole table would have gotten up and left and the holiday dinner would have been ruined. Why, oh why haven't I turned out like my mother? I wanted to, desperately. She seemed to me to sail through her life like an elegant swan—serene, intelligent, beautiful. She never argued with people, and yet she had strong opinions and beliefs which everyone who knew her honored.

Something wonderful has happened in Brussels. Phebe has finally gotten interested in money. She figures it constantly. I don't think she'll turn into a Common Market economist, though. Her remark about Brussels—"I adore it here. They really know what they're doing financially. They'll take American dollars, even in the smallest shops."

PHEBE

Joan is moaning here in this beautiful Brussels hotel room because she has caught her heel in the hem of her favorite skirt. "Now I'll have to troop around Paris, the fashion capital of the world, with a drooping hemline," she complains. I said I would be happy to fix it for her but I'd left my sewing kit at home. "You left it at home," she shrieked. "After all the trouble you went through to find the PERFECT sewing kit?" She was right. I had searched for the perfect sewing kit the way I'd shopped for the perfect luggage and the perfect clothes, often buying several suitcases and many clothing ensembles which turned out to be all wrong when I got them home.

The sewing kit dilemma was settled by the purchase of a tiny black nylon model of perfection. "You wouldn't even know it was a sewing kit," I said to Joan.

"Is there some reason you find it necessary to conceal the fact you have a sewing kit on your person?" she said. I came up with a rather lame answer. "Well, there is a folding scissors in this little pocket and someone might think I was hiding a dangerous weapon."

But the sewing kit is back in St. Paul on my dining room table, where I'd placed it to be sure I wouldn't forget to pack it. I asked her if by any chance she'd brought one. She was indignant. "You know I can't sew. I don't even own a sewing kit. I counted on you to bring yours." She continued. "You always do my sewing for me. I counted on you. After all, I'm doing the French—the least you could do is the sewing."

It's true. I always have done Joan's sewing for her. I used to say I was just showing her how to do it by having her watch me as I mended her seams, shortened her sleeve, repaired a zipper. But I finally gave in to doing it myself. She was so pathetic in her cunning, bringing out a little crumpled bunch of material, laying it out casually on the table as we sat in her kitchen drinking coffee and talking.

But once she went too far. One night around 8:30 just after all the kids were in bed, John was working late and I was reveling in my solitude, the doorbell rang. It was Doug with little Dennis in tow, holding up a little shirt. Doug spoke for him. "Joan said maybe you would be willing to sew on his Cub Scout badges." How could I say that the chapter of the *Iliad* I was reading was far too engrossing to put down? One of my neighborhood women friends had read Clifton Fadiman's list of the world's 100 best books and we had decided to make our days worthwhile by reading them all. These were IMPORTANT books that every educated person should read.

Or how could I explain to sweet little Dennis that I'd refused to let my own sons join Cub Scouts because I believed scouting encouraged militarism? I was trying to raise my sons to be peace loving, although it wasn't working well. Since I wouldn't buy them war toys, they bit their graham crackers into little guns and ran about the house shouting bang, bang at each other.

No, I couldn't explain all this to Joan's chubby cherub, face uplifted and expectant.

Was it his fault his mother didn't know how to sew? I took the shirt and diligently stitched the badges to the sleeve with tiny, taut stitches that no warlike rough-housing could dislodge.

Here in Brussels I look up from my journal and say to Joan, "Do you remember the time you tricked me into sewing on Dennis' Cub Scout badges?"

5. PICNIQUE IN PARIS
A moveable feast in a plastic sack

MAY 14
JOAN

On the Etoile du Nord: This is one of those trains you dream about, non-stop to Paris at over 100 miles per hour. We're swanking it up, alone in our first class compartment with etched glass doors, on our way to the City of Light, as Phebe keeps saying.

I want to see Paris in the light. I've only seen Paris through tears. It was one terrible spring after the death of my friend Merry, my divorce and the last days of a love so strong I was sure its ending must kill me.

But it hadn't. Love is hardly ever fatal no matter how much you want it to be at the time. And now here I am going back to Paris. I wonder if all my old sorrows will be there waiting for me.

These thoughts make me lonely for Bob. Homesickness may protect me from Paris. I'm going to write him a letter on the next page and then tear it out and mail it to him. It's defacing this perfect journal but I'll paste the page back in when I get home.

We looked out and there it was—Paris. The train arrived right on time at the Gare Nord which gave us the feeling that we would have a whole lovely day in Paris, starting immediately. Not so fast. First we got into an enormous, loud, quarrelsome, typically French line for cabs and then, after waiting a boring two hours for him, got the Driver From Hell. We very carefully arranged our trip with this maniac before we left the station. In our best mime, we showed him how cautiously we wanted him to drive us to our destination, the Hotel Grandes. We spread out our maps of Paris, marked to show the best route with hazards along the way prinked out in red. We had the exact change in francs for the ride and we cleverly showed him the three different tips we had at the ready, depending on how well he followed our directions.

None of it helped. In one of the busiest intersections in Paris, he stopped the cab, threw our bags into the street, demanded money and pointed us up an enormous hill, then sped away. We walked two long blocks uphill before we spotted the sign, GRANDES. Or rather GRAN, as the other letters had long since burned out. The Hotel Grandes was not a pretty sight and anything but grand.

PHEBE

The surly cab driver dropped us two blocks away from our hotel and over-charged us to boot. Surly is perhaps a word I'll use often in Paris, judging from my first two hours here. I'm determined not to be kept from the magic of "The City of Light," hard as it is to cling to optimism after viewing the seediness of our hotel. I pretended I thought it charming. "Oh, it's so Parisian!" I said, trying not to notice the incredible grime, the filthy and partially-ripped wallpaper, the foul-smelling bathroom. I even pretended the pillow was fine although it was harder than the rock Jacob slept on in the desert.

Now we're sitting on a bench in front of Notre Dame and I've just sketched a gorgeous, ornate street light. Every time I draw in my journal I realize how it helps me to better see all the exquisite details Paris is so justly famous for. I'm not good at drawing, but if I keep practicing, I'll get better. Even concert pianists have to practice six to eight hours a day, I heard once on public radio. This humble street lamp is a perfect example of the intense devotion to beauty I like to think is characteristic of Paris. But Joan says I must stop drawing because she is feeling faint from hunger.

I want to order something special for my first French meal. Joan says to order lamb chops and a salad, because those are the only two items she's sure she can translate. She's in charge of French since my only other language is Norwegian, a language not much in demand. Parisians seem proud of not knowing any language other than French. So Joan says we can't count on the waiter translating the other menu items. "We don't want to end up with something that turns out to be brains of a dead rabbit."

JOAN

At the Grandes Hotel: With a cold, sinking feeling in my stomach I remembered what one of my well-traveled pals told me before we left. She said, always, always, always ask to see the room before signing in with a hotel or giving them your passport, especially in lower-priced hotels. Yes, she said, it is embarrassing for Americans and it will be for you, the first time you try it. But all Europeans do it and hotel clerks will think you're a fool if you don't ask. Worse, they often give you a broom closet to sleep in if you don't ask first to see the room.

Phebe and I tried to buck each other up with a little positive thinking. "Oh, look, we've got a dear little balcony looking right out on the street." The balcony was tiny and a life-threatening maze of rust. The street scene was one long gray wall of the Gare St. Lazare, the only pedestrians some ladies of the night in hair curlers.

"Oh, my goodness, doesn't this orange and brown flowered wallpaper remind you of the fifties when these colors were all the rage?" The filth on the paper makes it obvious that it had been placed on the wall during the1950's and, not only not changed but, never washed since.

We opened the windows in our room to see if we could get the damp smell out. It was so fetid and rotten that it seemed no fresh air had penetrated this room since the Middle Ages. But as soon as we opened the windows, in flew thousands of tiny black bugs. They settled all over everything, especially the few dim lights in the room. We tried to shoo them back out to no avail, so they will share our humble digs tonight with us.

Ah well, sleep was out of the question anyway. The sheets are pale tan, but I'm sure they must have started life out as white, and the pillow on the old bed was one long sausage roll, hard as a rock, which they've stuck under the bottom sheet so they don't need a pillowcase.

MAY 15

PHEBE

This is Le Fleabag Hotel for sure. We have suffered and survived the night, despite the roaring sound of trains which seemed close enough to crash into our beds. I awoke often, needing to go to the bathroom, but afraid to. But then I

remembered my black nylon raincoat, which doubles as a robe. I thought it would make me look suitably sinister for the foray into the dark hallway. Who knew what evil lay in wait?

When I finally returned, unharmed, I lay awake, thinking of our door, which looked as though it had been kicked in several times and inadequately repaired. We'd pushed the chest of drawers against it, but would it hold? At least my travelers' checks were safe. I'd gone to bed with them neatly stuffed into my woolen socks, worn to avoid cold feet. Actually, I keep my checks in my socks by day, too. "Who would think to look there?" I asked Joan, pointing out how clever I was. "Who would want to look there?" Joan responded, with her usual candor.

Joan has decided we need to learn to use the Metro today. She's so confident, so game to try anything. I'm ashamed to admit I was going to suggest we simply walk or take taxis. I'm convinced it's her private Catholic big city school education that makes her so plucky and unafraid. Furthermore, she learned French. I grew up in a small town and never had a chance to take any language. My parents never spoke Norwegian in front of us kids. What little I knew as a child I learned from the old men lounging around the pool hall. I had to wait until I went to Augsburg College to take a class in Norwegian. Oh well. So what if I can't speak French? I'll just keep my mouth shut and let Joan talk.

JOAN

We decided to get right out into Paris this morning and scared and tired as we are, her beauty soon seduced us. We got our Orange Cards first. These are passes that will allow us to ride the Metro cheaply, a special deal for tourists. You need to have your picture on the card so we headed for a train station that is also a Metro station. We've noticed that these dual stations often have those coin-operated photo booths.

You need a lot of change to work these machines and the instructions are all in French and Arabic. Luckily, there were lots of young tourists from everywhere hanging around. Using mime and good will we all helped each other get our pictures taken. Phebe and I have used miming gestures several times already on this trip, whenever and wherever people didn't understand our language. This in spite of the fact that we both LOATHE mime. Hate to say it, but it works. The universal non-language. After our pictures were ready, we bought Metro Passes—La Carte Orange—and zipped right off to the Metro.

The Metro will take us everywhere. I know that once you get the hang of it, it's fantastically easy to use. I had to learn it all over again so I'm going to write it down this time. If, God willing, I ever get back to Paris, I'll be able to use the Metro fearlessly from the first day.

First, stations have huge maps everywhere and the different lines are color-coded. A train has the name of the last place they stop on the front of the engine. So you always know what direction it's going. Here's an example. Say the Metro has five stations—Apple-Bacon-Celery-Dill-Eggs. You are at the BACON station and you want to go to DILL. You look for a train labeled EGGS. Coming back home to BACON, you'll look for a train labeled APPLE. Phebe wants me to quit talking about it. "Don't give me that stupid example again," she said. "You've got me looking all over Paris for a Metro train labeled EGGS or APPLES."

We got off at the Ile de Cite where we meandered around bemused and excited. We're really in Paris, really, really. We tried to get into Ste. Chapelle, my favorite place in the world perhaps, but a very rude policeman stuck his baton in my ribs and told us to move on, move on.

Next we walked down to Notre Dame and the statue of Charlemagne on the Seine. We walked across the bridge and into the Rive Gauche where we immediately felt at home. It's near the Boul' Mich' and the Boul' St. Germaine with flowers, sidewalk cafes and young people kissing everywhere you look. Narrow, twisty streets and bookstores, bookstalls, books! We decide that this neighborhood is where we must live and plan to come back first thing in the morning and look for a new hotel.

Tonight the awful humor of our squalid digs strikes us. It really is the pits. The bathroom is down the hall, smells bad, and is so dirty that last night Phebe scrubbed the toilet before she felt she could use it. There was no hot water and she had to scrub in the dark, with only a pale light from the hall, as the bath light was burned out.

MAY 16

PHEBE

I'm sitting alone in a little park a few blocks from our new hotel, totally at peace with a serene stone statue for company. I can't quite decipher the name of the man but he seems to be a monk, judging from his clothing. E. Vil—no! It's F. Villon. Wonder if he's the poet. I'll check him out in this book I've just bought at the second-hand bookstore down the street, a book called *A Short History of French Literature* by Laurence Bisson. It says Villon

(1431-1463) was the first great French writer in the modern sense. I also learn that Villon once killed a man and therefore spent much of his life on the run. He frequently hid out in monasteries. So he was probably wearing a monk's robe as a disguise.

I love to be able to take time to go to bookstores, especially second hand ones, to sit around in parks and on benches outside buildings even when all Paris awaits. I love to meander without any plan or destination. I seem to fit the Pisces mold, dreamy and floaty. Joan, the Virgo, wants to make schedules and agendas for each day "so we don't waste time looking at or doing unimportant things we could just as well do at home," she says. I'm willing to have a schedule if we can occasionally ignore it. Now that I've got her writing in her journal almost more assiduously than I do, she's willing to put up with my unorganized ways.

I decided to go back and get Joan so I could show her the park and Villon's statue and read passages aloud to her from my book. "Are you turning into a Francophile?" Joan asked. I said maybe I was. At that moment I wished I'd chosen to spend part of my year off in Paris. Then Leah could have come over to visit. When she showed a talent for French in high school, my dream for her was that some day she'd study in Paris at the Sorbonne. Interesting how many of my ambitions involve living through other people. When I met John in college and realized he planned to be a college philosophy professor, I decided my ambition was to be a college professor's wife.

Aside from my ambitions for Leah and the Sorbonne, I've never been interested in French culture. Well, that's not entirely true. As young marrieds, when we read Sartre's *No Exit* in our Kenwood Playreading Group, I got interested in French Existentialism, at least on a superficial level. I thought it was funny to say I'd let John read all the deep philosophical tomes and I'd absorb them by sharing his bed. Actually, my interest was confined to wearing black Danskin tights and long black skirts with black turtle-neck tops. I'd learned about the Existentialists' attire when a friend went to Paris the summer I was in Norway. Paris sounded much more interesting than Oslo, where my Aunt Johanna was apt to drop in on me at any time and find me in the arms of my Norwegian boyfriend, almost ready to go "all the way."

JOAN

We get up and out as soon as it's light. The very first hotel on our list near the Sorbonne is a winner. The pretty receptionist is friendly and speaks English. The lobby is spacious, beautifully decorated. Our room is deluxe beyond dreaming. New plumbing in our own small, clean bathroom. Two huge windows on the street. A wonderful Left Bank neighborhood with winding streets, chimney pots, lots of flowers, a little park on the corner, a bistro across the way. We're about six blocks from Notre Dame, one block from the Sorbonne, two blocks from an open air food market and a Metro station. We feel as though we've stumbled into heaven, a heaven we can afford! I'm so overcome, I try to tell the maid, six-feet tall, black and beautiful, that I love the hotel, but in my poor French, what I actually say is that I love her. She laughs and laughs and then helps me with my pronouns.

We're off to the Metro and Tuileries Gardens, a wonderful park full of statues, adorable French children and those wonderful benches and wrought iron chairs that are so chic and Gallic. It starts to rain but we put up our umbrellas, wind our scarves around our hair and keep on walking. Rain doesn't send people indoors or to their cars in Paris today. This is a soft, misting rain that turns the streets into colored abstracts and puts halos around the lights.

We walk up the Champs-Elysees. By now it's raining harder so I try to talk Phebe into not stopping at every single statue, every window. She's in one of her "God is in the details" moods during which she insists on looking at every bloody thing she passes, sometimes even blades of grass or small bugs, through a dimestore magnifying glass she carries everywhere with her. Unfortunately, the statue I try to pry her away from is an important memorial and very beautiful too. "Art is my life, Joan," she intones and I am caught once more, doing the Philistine bit.

Our moods lift miraculously at the sight of a Burger King dead ahead. We race each other in for our first taste of home in over a week. I do feel bad that our culture has brought Burger King and McDonald's to this famous street but I can't help feeling joy too. This is a real Coke, real fries, real USA burgers with everything on them.

Then on to the Tomb of the Unknown Soldier. It's very moving, covered with flowers, an enormous French flag whipping in the breeze over it. We spend a long, long time here, just sitting and then writing in our journals. Journal writing is a wonderful excuse to sit down, take things slower, yet keep yourself looking somewhat busy while you travel. People leave you alone when you're writing in a journal and don't seem to begrudge you the long use of a bench.

PHEBE

Joan says I should go to the top of the Eiffel Tower, despite
my fear of heights. We had a gorgeous walk down the
Champs-Elysees. Little side parks along the way filled with
flowers and statues and fountains, all of which I wanted to
linger over.

We finally arrived at the Eiffel Tower. What I really
wanted to do was wait below while she went up, but before
I quite knew what had happened, we had bought tickets to
go to the highest ascension. Now I'm glad I went because it
was spectacular, although I could never bring myself to lean
on the railing and look over. What is this overwhelming fear
I've always had that I might jump off bridges or out of open
windows in high buildings?

I remember when I was single, teaching in a small town
high school how eager I was to get away each weekend. I was
dating one of the other teachers and once we came down to
"The Cities" together. We'd booked hotel rooms, separate
rooms, of course, in downtown Minneapolis. Staying in a
hotel seemed so glamorous and worldly. I was used to a small,
sparsely furnished bedroom in the house where I boarded with
two other female high school teachers.

That weekend was my first experience with drinking too
much. After we'd had dinner with several martinis (I had no
knowledge of the potency of martinis), I said I had to go back
to my hotel room because I was feeling sick. The room was
beastly hot and I pushed up the window as high as it would
go, then leaned out to feel the soothing cool of spring evening
air. I had forgotten I was on the fifth floor. When I looked
down, a dreadful dizziness overwhelmed me and a feeling
of guilt because I'd broken the pledge I'd taken in the Loyal
Temperance Legion when I was 10, never to let liquor touch
my lips. I also felt sad because during the entire weekend
my date had never once tried to kiss me. After Norway the
summer before, I'd come to expect men to make every attempt
to bed me. My task, of course, was to resist.

Now I wondered if I'd become unappealing to men. Perhaps it was because I'd gained at least twenty pounds after being fed all summer Norwegian delicacies like romegrot (cream pudding) and pastries whose main ingredient was butter. It didn't occur to me that Norwegian men might be sexually much less repressed than American men. And it certainly didn't occur to me that my date might be gay. Months later in a painful scene at the end of the school year, he announced that he was. In those unenlightened years of the 1950's, all I felt was disappointment and sadness.

But leaning out the hotel window that spring evening, nauseated from too many martinis, sick at heart with guilt,

filled with the sadness of my life, I simply thought: maybe I should just jump. Ever since I've had this overwhelming fear of heights.

JOAN

Evening-Eiffel Tower: Phebe finally conquers her fear of heights, and game little critter that she is, agrees to go up in the Tower, being more afraid, as she says, of missing a Peak Experience. So we go all the way up, to the 3rd Etarge.

We have timed our arrival here to be as near sundown as we could. So first we see Paris in a beautiful, fading twilight and then glowing as the sky darkens and all her evening lights come on.

We have trouble finding a Metro station close to the Eiffel Tower, must have walked out the wrong way. So we have a very long and lonely walk through scruffy parts of Paris before we find the Metro. We're both really exhausted by the time we get home and Phebe is in a terrible state because she has walked holes in some of her traveler's checks.

Incredible as it sounds, she decided to keep her unspent checks safe by putting them in a plastic bag inside her stockings and shoes. She walked on them all day long. Not only are there holes through two $50 checks but there's also green grunge imbedded in her feet from the plastic bag and two rather large and very green blisters on her heels.

Once we're done laughing, we can see that there's enough left of the checks to get a refund. So it isn't a real tragedy. Then I help Phebe soak her sore feet in the wastebasket.

PHEBE

Here I am lying on the floor of our cozy hotel bathroom. I've brought in my pillow and blanket and my book because I'm desperately sick with an attack of indigestion. I can't sleep and I don't want to turn on any lights that might wake up Joan.

I worried when I first separated from John: how could I live alone? What if I got sick in the middle of the night? Who would take me to the hospital? Then I remembered that when I was in my thirties, during the years I had three young children and a series of foster children, I'd often wake up at 2 am, certain I was going to die. Years later I realized that I was suffering from panic attacks. We had no name for them then, no treatment. I'd write long farewell letters to my relatives and friends, letters I always tore up in the morning. But when I was writing them I was convinced I was about to die. I couldn't breathe. Somehow the act of writing calmed me a little.

I'd never wake up John to ask him to comfort me. I'd tried that once and knew too well how impatient he'd be. "Go back to sleep. There's nothing wrong with you. You're perfectly healthy." So I figured out ways to handle my attacks alone, because I'd come to be ashamed of them after his initial reaction. I certainly wasn't going to tell anyone else about them. Sometimes I'd go down to the kitchen and fill a scrub pail full of hot water and ammonia. Then I'd scour the floor and a few whiffs of those powerful ammonia fumes would ease my anxiety.

There's precious little floor to scrub here and no ammonia in sight, so guess I'll try writing. No farewell letters to friends. I've outgrown them. Instead I'll try a few affirmations: God is healing me now. God is healing me now. God is healing me now.

MAY 17

JOAN

Dawn: Phebe woke me up during the night with her stomach pains and I woke up this morning with cystitis. One of my worst fears is upon me—sick to the point of needing a doctor in a foreign city with only high school French from long ago to help me. Thank God Phebe is with me as my very worst fear has always been that I will die all alone somewhere. And I used to worry, when I was single, about being buried alone, with no one lying next to me for eternity. I know that's a stupid and unimportant worry but it's the kind I brood about.

After Merry died, the thing that woke me night after night was so small compared to the loss and grief I felt during the day. I would wake, sick with fear, wondering if Merry's feet had been cold as she was dying. I didn't know if she had been wearing a warm robe or slippers when she hanged herself in that cold garage. Such a small, homely, everyday worry but it has given me a wound that I fear will never heal.

PHEBE

I awoke, hungry and raring to go to breakfast, but Joan wasn't. She'd been awake half the night because her back hurt. "Guess I'm just sore from all the walking we did yesterday. I have to go back to bed for a little while." So unlike her. She's never sick.

But soon she said she was ready for breakfast. I could tell she still wasn't feeling like herself, though, and as we walked down the street to a cafe, she admitted she was in serious pain. "Maybe I have a bladder infection." Almost as soon as she said it, I saw a sign on the wall of the building we were passing. "I think it says doctor's office," I said. Maybe I know more French than I think. After all, I did take Latin in high school.

Now here we sit in the waiting room. The doctor has just come up to us and said in perfect English, "I can receive you now if you want." Joan must have been feeling really awful to agree to come in here, because she hates to break down and see a doctor almost as much as I do. In my family we never called a doctor unless my mother was going to have a baby or someone had a serious disease like pneumonia, which killed my baby brother John Phillip.

I hope all this doctor has to do is simply prescribe a medicine and soon Joan will be good as new. I hope she doesn't have to go to a hospital. I hope I don't have to call Bob and tell him Joan is seriously ill with some terrible kidney disease. I must stop creating these worst case scenarios. Breathe deeply. Calm down. Ah, here she is now, all smiles. No need to call Bob. No need to arrange for dialysis. No need to look for a suitable kidney donor without any French to plead in. No need to worry about how to ship her dead body home.

JOAN

On a quay across from Notre Dame: We're enjoying the most marvelous picnic of crusty bread, runny cheese, and water as we watch the boats sailing up and down the Seine and gaze our fill at the magnificent cathedral across from us. The sun is lovely, just warm enough, and I feel wonderful, knowing that I will not be shut up in a Paris hospital after all.

By the most incredible chance, Phebe spotted a gynecologist's office on our way to the Metro this morning. I was just going to wait and see if I felt better, but she muscled me through the office door.

At first, I thought it was in vain. "Je suis malade," I kept repeating to the obviously frightened receptionist. This was, I think, because I was saying "I am bad" rather than "I feel bad." Finally, she fled and a moment later, the doctor appeared and in perfect English asked me how he could help. Turns out he's a teacher in the medical school at the Sorbonne and was anxious to try out his English as he was soon to appear at an International OB/GYN Conference.

After a very thorough examination, the doctor presented me with two kinds of medicine (125f) and his bill for services (150f). I don't think I'll ever be frightened of getting sick in a foreign land again. Being in the neighborhood of the University was certainly a help.

After lunch, we crossed the bridge and after admiring the carved doors and famous gargoyles, entered Notre Dame. Right now, we are sitting down and writing in our journals in front of a 14th century statue of Our Lady in the transept of the cathedral. In back and in front of us are the incredible rose windows, which I remember Mom saying were saved from the bombs in World War II by being removed and taken to caves in the countryside. All around us, tourists are hurrying in and out. They're taking dozens of pictures and then rushing out to catch their tour bus before it leaves. But Phebe and I, feeling blessed by our own slower pace, sit in a little oasis of peace and quiet and write devotedly.

I just lit candles and cried a bit for my parents. I can't seem to shake the sadness, the feeling of being an orphan that I've had ever since my father died. At my age, isn't this silly, pathetically silly? When will I ever really feel like an adult? I've lived now for over half a century and still feel like a child. It's no use. I can't shame myself into feeling grown-up. I can't talk myself out of feeling lonely and abandoned.

PHEBE

We're having lunch on a wooden park bench along the Seine across from Notre Dame. We've each bought a large bottle of Coke and one of water, part of our new decision to drink frequently. I also ate a banana, a piece of seriously crusty, dense bread, and a container of yogurt—all good for my digestion, I hope.

Bearing the remnants of lunch and newly-filled water bottles, we come to Notre Dame to gaze upon the miracle of this building's interior. There are wooden carvings of the life of Christ—Mary and Elizabeth and little figures of local people. Here's a 14th century statue of the Virgin entitled "Our Lady of Paris." She's holding Baby Jesus in her left hand and a lily in her right. The entire statue is supported on the back of a bare-breasted mermaid. An odd touch. Here's the incomparable rose window, as Michelin says, "...so perfect that it has never shifted in over 700 years..."

We've walked to the Ste. Chapelle, a "Gothic marvel" and are now on the upper level where hordes of school children are gathered in little tour groups. The windows here are breathtaking. Each of the sections is enclosed by gilt-painted wooden frames, which reflect the light and make the room glow.

I want to come back someday. There it is—that odd phenomenon I experience so often. I find a place which affects me deeply and I immediately say, "Oh, I must come back some day." As if I can't take time right now to fully appreciate it.

JOAN

Ste. Chapelle: It's as beautiful as my memory of it, as lovely as being inside a multi-colored Christmas ornament looking out. I look for an omen, a sign like the one I had the last time I sat here. Then I had lit a candle for my friend, but a gust of wind caught at it and it went out, like a life does sometimes, all at once. Like Merry's life, too cruel to go on, too young to end. I had lit candle after candle for her all across France that spring... in great cathedrals, small towns, wayside shrines. Until one day in Paris, here in the Ste. Chapelle, when I lit the candle, it glowed and grew. And at that very moment, the rain stopped and the sun came in through these incredible windows and I felt the first hope in months that she was alive. Somewhere. Not doomed, at all.

Today I look up and see that the sun is shining through one pane of glass so clearly, a picture of Mary and Joseph. Looking for comfort, I imagine this is a sign that my parents are still somehow looking after me from beyond wherever they've gone. I feel my sadness lift, almost as swiftly and cleanly as it did that spring years ago.

This place will always seem to me the holiest of places. Today, even with the seats blocked off so that Phebe and I must sit on the stone floor to write in our journals and with groups of school children running up and down the stairs, it is still such hallowed ground.

Coming out of church and down to earth, we are somewhat frantic for a bathroom and neither of us has the necessary francs to unlock the one in the square. We decide to visit a nearby restaurant, order frugally a small cake and tea each and then use their bathroom. The bill is $12. I blame Phebe for this although I don't say so out loud. She insists that my bladder infection is due to an inadequate daily amount of water and forces it down my throat often from the large bottles of Evian water that she makes me carry everywhere.

Back to the hotel for a little rest. We've brought supper, crusty bread, fresh vegetables and fruit, some cheese, and also a bouquet of pale, golden-apricot tulips which makes our lovely room even lovelier.

MAY 18

PHEBE

Today we took the metro to the Montmartre district and the Basilica of the Sacred Heart. I've been fascinated by the

Sacred Heart ever since that day when my Catholic friend and I were playing with our Shirley Temple paper dolls up in her bedroom. I noticed a picture on her wall, a picture of Jesus. But it wasn't like Salman's "Head of Christ" I was used to. This picture showed Jesus's heart as a fat red blob on the outside of his garment. (We always called the clothes Biblical characters wore garments.)

"Why is His heart on the outside of His body?" I, the innocent Lutheran, asked.

"Because it's the Sacred Heart," she said, "and that's why it has a glow around it, too. To show it's special." Our town was named Sacred Heart. Population 792 with four Lutheran churches, despite its name. My friend's family were the only Catholics. There must have been more Catholics at some point because the town was named by a Jesuit priest, ministering to fur traders and Native Americans in the 19th century.

So here I am in a church in Paris named after my home town, and Joan discourages me from going inside. "It's of little historic importance," she insists, refusing to join me in my pilgrimage. I go in by myself, leaving her to wander around alone. Inside I find a little slip of paper in English giving me all sorts of important information I'd think a devout Catholic like Joan would be happy to have.

The church was built to accomplish a vow made during the year 1870 when the Franco-Prussian War was raging. St. Theresa of the Infant Jesus, the poet Max Jacob, and the painter Utrillo often prayed here. So while Joan is poking about the evil streets, I sit here piously copying down Catholic information she should be attending to. I've agreed to join her later in Pigalle, even though I'm afraid of what is there. Raw sex and pornography scare me.

But here in this church I feel safe, protected, valued. All who walk in and see me writing so steadfastly in my journal will smile benevolently and give me their silent blessing as they pass. No need to worry here about the dark power of sex, about "Playboys" and "Hustlers" and ragged paperbacks with their covers torn off, hidden under the cushions of overstuffed chairs.

JOAN

Since I was last in Montmarte, they've added a funicular right along the side of the long stairs to Sacre Coeur. It's lots of fun and the price of the ride is included in our Orange Cards. Phebe wants to go into the church but I don't, so I wander up to the Place de la Tertes. The square is clanking with tourists and pretty bad art which they are buying as fast as they can get their credit cards out of their wallets. Lots of photo scene paintings of Montmartre and portraits of those little kids with the big, diseased-looking eyes. Nothing I can imagine anyone actually hanging up at home. But it's fun and colorful. Phebe joins me full of her visit to Sacre Coeur. She can't understand

why I didn't go in with her. I tell her that Catholics have no more need to go in every Catholic Church they pass than Lutherans have to tack up 95 Theses on every Catholic Church door. This silences her for a moment and on we wander.

We visit a house, now a café, where Dufy, Utrillo, Renoir and Suzanne Valladon, mother of Utrillo, all painted. Then we stop at the Lapin Agile, a cafe that has hosted literary evenings every week for 800 years. Next a long, long cold walk looking for the cemetery where many famous Parisians and Jimmy Hendrix are said to be buried. We never do find it and after what seems hours of walking, I finally talk Phebe into getting on the Metro and heading for Pigalle.

What a disappointment. It's a small version of Times Square, dirty, full of unimaginative sex shows, shops and gaudy souvenirs. Boring really. I think people fighting sex education in schools should reconsider. If we really want to cut down on teen sex, let's force kids to attend every boring sex show we can find and read every poorly-written porno book. They'll lose interest in sex for life. Like my friend, a single mom, who tried hard to use modern sex education guides with her son until one day he said, "Oh, Mom, not that boring old intercourse stuff again." So much for thoroughly modern mothering.

We have to change trains at St. Lazare so I stop and try to validate my Eurail Pass. The clerk is sullen and unsmiling until she figures that she isn't going to have to do anything for me after all. I don't have my passport with me so she won't have to validate my pass. Now she's all smiles, seems to be really enjoying turning me down. Clerks can be petty tyrants the world over. And who wouldn't become one if they had to deal with the public all day? I certainly would.

I was fired from my very first real job, because I couldn't stomach being nice all day. It was early one Sunday morning. I was a 16-year-old soda jerk who had been out late the night before and was in no mood to serve my public with a smile. In walked, what seemed to my young and slim self, a very Fat Lady. She was probably twenty pounds lighter than I am right now. She had the NERVE to ask for a banana split early on a Sunday morning when the correct call would be for the Sunday paper, black coffee and a Bromo. But I made the disgusting thing and when I put it down in front of her, she had the gall to whine, "Miss, you forgot the banana."

I looked. It was true. There was no banana under the three mounds of ice cream, three heaping toppings, nuts, whipped cream, cherries. So I walked over, tore a banana off the bunch and slapped it down on the counter in front of the Fat Lady. "Here," I said, "here's your banana." She went directly to the manager who came directly to me, demanding an immediate apology. I refused. Immediate end of job.

I suppose this means a career in public service is out for me. It also cancels out Travel Agent—I would have to actually deal with people and they might not always do as they were told or go where I wanted them to go. It also finishes my dream of being the perfect Restaurant Hostess. When I remember some of the complaints I've made in restaurants over the years, it makes my blood run chill to think of having to be on the receiving end of them.

PHEBE
(VERSAILLES)

We had a 15-minute train ride through charming French villages with lots of stone and stucco houses. Years ago I visited a friend in a small town on the Minnesota-South Dakota border. We went for a walk so she could show me the town's most unusual sight, an elaborate chateau of pale yellow stucco, set amidst the plain white frame houses built by Scandinavian immigrants. The story was that a World War I veteran had fallen in love while stationed in France. His beloved didn't want to leave France, so he'd built this chateau for her, hoping to lure her to join him. She refused, and he lived alone in the house for the rest of his days. After he died, the chateau stood empty.

A dog is barking right here in the cafe. An unmistakable French bark. Coarser, more nasal somehow than an American dog's bark. Perhaps dogs and cats try to imitate the language they hear. The cat I heard meowing the other day inside a little box a woman was carrying on the Metro sounded different, too. What's different is that a dog is allowed in the cafe at all. I remember in Brussels, a woman sitting next to us had her little dog on her lap while she ate dinner. Unheard of in Minnesota restaurants.

I've just written postcards to my family telling them about Amsterdam. Yes, I'm a few cities behind, unlike Joan who seems to keep up. I'm reminded of the summer I spent a whole month at the North Shore all by myself, staring out at Lake Superior and writing poems on my old blue Smith Corona. Rolf wrote that everyone was waiting for a letter or at least a card from me. Then he signed it: "Keep in touch. Your son, Rolf."

JOAN
(VERSAILLES)

As soon as we arrived, we looked for a cafe to have a coffee. Why rush to the 9:45 tour, indeed why rush at all? That's our motto.

We find a wonderful neighborhood brasserie, full of life and fun. It's still breakfast time. I go up to the counter to get the coffees and stand next to a middle-aged woman with three glasses of wine lined up in front of her. She's very respectable looking, perhaps on her way to work. Won't she start the day with a real buzz on? I would.

We drink everything standing up. For some reason, anything liquid costs more in Paris if you sit down at a table. When we're good and rested, we take the King's Tour. The Castle is so huge, my feet start hurting just looking at it. Inside it's also strangely empty and tacky. All the furniture, it seems, was looted and/or burned during the Revolution and the French historical society people are really taking their time replacing it.

In the Hall of Mirrors or in one of the furnished bedrooms, you get a glimpse of what it must have been like for the Sun Kings and their queens. It's no wonder they lost their heads. It's too much, dear boy, much too much, as Tyrone Guthrie is reported to have said after watching an over-emoting actor in rehearsal.

At lunch, Phebe bought one piece of butter and a small salad in the Palace Restaurant and then proceeded to bring out her own yogurt and cheese. I'm embarrassed and point out the signs everywhere that clearly say "NO PICNIQUES." Phebe said, "This is no picnic, this is hard work" and proceeded to pull out a 1.5 liter bottle of water. I laughed so hard! Then she stole a spoon. I saw her do it.

PHEBE

I could sit dreaming in this café for hours, watching people and writing in my journal. Details of ordinary life, which I love more than anything. The sudden glimpse of a pocket-sized courtyard through a doorway in a high fence. A whole life going on inside, a woman from another century, one of Monet's women, in a long skirt and apron, bent over her flowers, digging in the dirt. I remember my mother in her apron, one of those practical aprons she would automatically fling over her head every morning. A soft cotton apron sprinkled with tiny flowers and decorated with faded rickrack. How good it was to bury my head in that apron, lean into her sweet breasts while she comforted me because two of my friends had refused to let me make mudpies with them. I'd heard one of their mothers call out the back door to them as I walked up the sidewalk in front of her house. "Here comes that Phebe Dale. Now don't let her boss you around." Oh, early childhood loss of innocence. To think that someone didn't love me as my mother did.

Now here in France thousands of miles away from home and childhood, I want to call out to Joan to look at the Monet woman in her homely apron. Or maybe I'd say as Colette would have, her favorite word: "Regarde! Regarde!" How surprised Joan would be to hear me speak French aloud.

We decided to take a little lunch break at the museum cafeteria. I chose the crudites raw carrots, beets, and maybe turnips. Or could they possibly be rutabagas, Swedish turnips, much-served and often-moaned-over vegetable of my childhood? My father grew them in his garden and my mother cooked them until they were soft, then whipped them together with cream and butter. The vegetables today weren't cooked and mashed but raw and chopped. Each morsel had absorbed flavors of herbs and vinegar and olive oil. Besides the vegetables, I took a pat of butter for the bread and cheese I'd so cleverly secreted in my ubiquitous plastic shopping bag. I'm rather proud of myself for having come up with this idea, taking extras from the table whenever we eat out. I think it's a habit that will come in handy when I'm old and poor. Guess I've always had this belief that someday I'd end up very poor, perhaps even a bag lady, surviving on the leavings of others.

I also stole a spoon from the cafeteria, and I hope Joan didn't notice. I've had urges before to steal small items from public places, but I've never actually done it. Maybe instead of a bag lady, I'll turn into a kleptomaniac and my children will have to "put me away." My Swedish grandmother was "put away" after my grandfather died because she fell apart. The only time I went to see her, she wept bitterly when it was time for me to go, begging me not to leave her, stroking my hands, kissing me over and over. My grandmother was seven years older than my grandfather, a fact I learned as a very young child, perhaps from my father. He often made fun of my grandmother, partly because she could neither read nor write, not even in Swedish. But mostly I think because of the age difference between her and my grandfather. Somehow that seemed ludicrous to him. I think it still does to many. If the man is older, that's normal, but not if the woman is the older one.

MAY 20

JOAN

Today we spent the day in the ugly, fascinating Georges-Pompidou, the place for modern art in Paris. Outside, a glass escalator takes us to the top of the building for a fantastic view of the city. The building is constructed with an overlay of colored pipes and lights.

The square in front of the museum is full of kids and amazing and funny street acts. Inside there are three full rooms of Matisse! And every other famous artist of our century too, it seems. But I'm too tired to enjoy it. I'm so tired I can't even think about it. All I can do is think crossly that they should have put in more BENCHES. My back hurts and I want to sit down. And I want to go home.

This naturally leads me straight down that old street Self-Pity where I wallow around asking myself , "Where is my real home now that I'm an orphan?" and "What will become of me without a job?" and "Why I am I wandering around Europe happy and unaware while at home my old life may be unraveling?"

PHEBE

The Pompidou is a wild and crazy museum with a fantastic glass escalator attached to the outer wall of the building. We have ascended in that open glass escalator up to the top, five stories high, and I wasn't even afraid. This is better than the Eiffel Tower. Even though we can't see as far, we can see more clearly, because we're closer to the ground. Why do we think the higher we get the better? Five stories is plenty high. Safer, too, since I read once that most fire ladders only reach five stories. Good thing I didn't think of that fact when we were rising to the top of the Eiffel Tower.

Funny how the brain calls forth such facts when you don't really want them. However, I often can't remember the plot of a book I read only a few weeks ago. Or the name of an old and dear college friend when I run into her at Southdale, even though she immediately calls me by name the moment I see her.

I'm standing now in front of a painting by a Swiss artist, Eva Aeppli Zofingen, born in 1925. The painting is called "Groupe de 13" and shows thirteen women in olive-green velvet gowns. They are tall and skinny, with long, cadaver-like hands.

I often notice hands more than anything else. What do I remember most about my mother? How her hands looked as she lay in her casket, which was in our living room for a whole day before the funeral. Even though I was told not to go in there, I sneaked in and pushed a chair up so I could get a good look at her. Then I made the mistake of reaching over and stroking her hands. They were so cold and hard. That's when I realized she was really dead.

MAY 21

JOAN

We were taught never to lie by the nuns but sometimes it's necessary, isn't it? I remember Sister St. Joan in sixth grade when the war was over and we knew all about the atrocities and concentration camps. When Sister said there was never a reason to lie, I stuck my hand up.

"Sister, what if there was a Nazi at the door," I said, "and what if he asked you if you were hiding a Jewish family and you were? Would you give them up?"

"Of course not," Sister said, "When the Nazi soldier asked me if there were any Jews here, I would look down the sleeve of my habit and say, 'No, there are no Jews in here.' This would be no lie. There would be no Jews up my sleeve." Sometimes I think I never tell the absolute truth to anyone. Maybe this is where it started. And maybe it's not such a bad thing.

This morning I walked four or five blocks to a post office and on the way back, got lost. Then I decided you can't be really lost in Paris, everything here is too interesting. I stopped for two cups of strong French coffee, standing up in a working man's bar with the men from the markets in their blue coveralls. Then I roamed aimlessly until I spotted a landmark and wended my way home.

After a nice, long rest, we're shopping in Paris this afternoon at the Palais Royal and delight in the arches and gardens and all the wonderful little shops along the sides. The Palais Royal we learn was built for Richelieu but it seems too enormous to have ever been a private residence. We find some beautiful, ancient medals, four different kinds with lions. Bob collects lions and I think he should love these medals on his Greek fisherman's cap.

After shopping, we sit in the square, getting the good out of the sunny day. Paris is full of wonderful little squares, fountains, beautiful statues and lots of places to sit and read or write in your journal. Or kiss. My goodness there's a lot of serious kissing going on in Paris. I love to see this, reminds me of my dating days when we would neck in parked cars. We called it watching the Submarine Races when we parked down at Lake Harriet. Serious kissing with just a little bit of petting. I never considered going "all the way." I might have told friends it was because of my strict Catholic school upbringing but the truth of the matter was it was my selfishness. I wasn't going to trade in my virginity until I got something for it.

The government is doing something terrible here. Right in front of the Comedie Francais they are filling the courtyard with ugly black and white columns of different heights. The people of Paris obviously hate it. They have written many messages on the board fence around the construction site. My favorite says—"Why not put a punk hairdo on La Jaconda (the Mona Lisa) while you're at it, Minister of Culture?"

How amazing and wonderful to be in a country that takes beauty so seriously that even their graffiti concerns itself with it. Unlike America, where most of our graffiti is about bodily functions, especially the pleasurable ones.

PHEBE

I dreamt about my grandparents last night. My grandmother was born in small village in Smaland, of peasant stock, had never been able to go to school, never learned to read or write. I remember how she loved to shop, especially at the Glass Block department store in downtown Duluth. She had to sign the charge slip with a large shaky X. I was often ashamed of her. Now I realize how little I really knew her and have an enormous desire to know more. Why am I only going to Norway where my father came from? Why am I not going to Sweden, too? I want to find her home town. I want to look up my grandfather's relatives, if there are any left in Stockholm. Another story I heard as a child was that my grandfather was from a finer family than my grandmother. His two older spinster sisters highly disapproved of the marriage. When my mother was four and her brother Harry was six my grandparents decided to emigrate to America, maybe to avoid the disapproving sisters.

My grandparents have been dead for over forty years, yet I think of them often and feel regret I failed to ask them about their lives. Often I dream of them. They're living in Duluth, are young and beautiful and very happy. In the dream I always say, "I didn't know you were still alive. Now I'll come see you often."

MAY 22
JOAN

THE LOUVRE: Too much, too big, too rich. As Phebe said, "They don't have the good sense to put a few things away in storage. They must have everything they own out on show."

We walk miles and everything blurs. I read somewhere about a guidebook that claimed you could see the entire Louvre in four hours and told you just what to look at and what not. This amused some French art students so much that they did their own tour of the Louvre on roller blades and then wrote an article about doing the Louvre in 30 minutes. I know it was a joke, but right now I wish I had some other means of propelling myself through the museum than just my old feet.

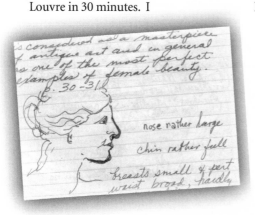

We started with the Venus de Milo and spent quite a bit of time examining her. For one thing, she's about ten feet tall. When you first see her you think— perfection. She has those little, saucy, upturned breasts I've always wanted. She also has perfect feet which I don't have either.

There are just plain too many paintings here, room after red room. You get jaded, sated. And they hang them one atop the other way up to the very high ceiling. You'd have to lie on your back on the floor to really see the top ones.

Huge crowds in front of the Mona Lisa, pushing and shoving to get a better look. Yet near it is another famous DaVinci, a Madonna, and next to that Raphael's Holy Family. Across the way a gorgeous Caravaggio. No one is paying the slightest bit of attention to any of them.

We are overcome with weariness and stop for coffee after which we just race through room after room. We have become art zombies. I tell Phebe— "walk faster, don't look, it's nobody." Then I see to my shame that I have hustled her right by a room full of paintings by Franz Hals.

6. CROSSING THE ALPS
Wearing all the wrong clothes

MAY 23

PHEBE
(TRAIN TO LAUSANNE)

A few minutes ago, I was about to blow up my white plastic inflatable neck pillow when Joan complained. "It's embarrassing to have one's chosen traveling companion blowing up what looks like a giant oddly-shaped balloon. It looks like one of those doughnut pillows people use to ease the pain of hemorrhoids."

"Speaking of hemorrhoids," I said, "I could use one of those pillows, too. Do you think we can find one in Lausanne?" The thought of miming our request to the man in the medical supply store set us to laughing. Joan stopped complaining about my neck pillow. I continued to blow it up, determined to catch a little nap. As soon as she saw me dozing, she said, "OK, so you don't mind sleeping right through Corot country."

Out our train window, I get a glimpse of a man sowing seeds, scattering them from a blue pouch slung around his waist, just like in the days of yore. It's these sudden little images I love, these tiny scenes that flash by and make me realize I'm not in America, but in Europe.

Now we're climbing fast. Joan goes on with her travel commentary. "There, Phebe. You've just seen your first Alp!" I am seized with an insane desire to minimize the mountains, to say, "Oh, they're nothing compared to the mountains of Norway. You should see the mountains my father came from in Dale, his little hometown. Besides, there are fjords in Norway, something you don't have here on the Continent. Too bad you refused to travel to Norway with me. Then you'd really see mountains."

I remember how terrifying I found those mountains when I spent the summer of 1950 in Norway as a student. My Aunt Johanna took me on a boat and train tour.

Sometimes we had to take little buses because the narrow hairpin-curved roads were only single lane. I remember well the time our bus met another and there was agitated discussion between the bus drivers as to who should back down or up the mountain to let the other pass. My fear of heights was probably at its most intense during that little encounter.

I grew up surrounded by wide prairie farmlands. I could relate to what a friend of mine said after her first mountain sighting, "Well, they're OK, but they get in the way of the view." I was used to vast sky and a blessed horizon. Years later I found out Emerson understood. He once wrote: "The health of the eye demands a horizon."

JOAN

I'm sitting in the sun in the garden of the Hotel le Chalet in Lausanne, Switzerland. This is a charming hotel with the motto carved right into its wooden face QUE LA PAIX SOIT CETTE MAISON. That's certainly true. It drips peace here. The garden is breaking out in a paintbox of color—iris, tulips, jonquils, geraniums. The peonies are swollen and ready to burst, too. I'm clean as a whistle after my bath (3f. a bain) and I'm sitting and drying my hair and resting.

Phebe has gone on a quest to the Old Town to see Rue Edward Gibbon and the cathedral Gibbon wrote about so lovingly in his autobiography she's reading. She's fascinated by the fact that he converted from Episcopalian to Catholic and back to Episcopalian when his father blew a gasket over his turning Catholic. It occurs to me he must have been a Grade A Wimp. He also broke off his engagement to the girl of his dreams because his father objected to her, on the grounds she had no money. Well, was his father wrong. That girl went on to become Madame Necker, wife of the Minister of Finance in Paris, famous for her hospitality, intelligence and beauty.

Actually, reading Gibbon here does make sense. I wish I had brought more literature of the places we're seeing. It would be fun to read what Lord Byron or Dickens had to say about Lausanne right while I'm here.

Our morning was hard. We started late in Paris. We were finally awakened at 6 am with little mews from our teeny, tiny traveling alarm clock. The hotel failed to call us at 5:45 and they hadn't ordered a taxi for us either. When they did, it arrived in five minutes, before we were ready, so we had a mad dash to pack, clean ourselves up a bit and get to the station. My bag has gotten so heavy, it's killing me. The train station, this early, was a madhouse. But train travel does make life civilized. We did have time for some coffee before our 7:14 am train and loved the swirl of people around us as we drank.

The train times are a hoot. 7:14, not 7:10 or 7:15. And you can bet your last dollar that 7:14 is exactly when the train will pull out of the station. The trains are all wonderful but the one this morning was really special, the famous TGV from Paris to Switzerland, 160 miles per hour with the smoothest ride you can imagine.

We were glad we had saved French francs as souvenirs this morning instead of trading them all in for Swiss money. No one told us that when you travel from one country to the next, you'll need money of the country you're leaving. For instance, going from Paris to Lausanne, only French francs were accepted on the train.

Phebe slept a bit, which was a shame because every view out of the train window, as we left Paris for the countryside, seemed to me to be a landscape by Corot.

PHEBE

We arrived on the dot of 11:10, just as we were told in Paris we would. Immediately, as if by magic, we found a luggage cart, an ever-more important amenity as our backs continue to age, even as we travel. I changed my traveler's checks into Swiss francs, smug Joan having already done hers back in the USA. Now Joan is waiting in line to make reservations for our train to the Cinque Terre, which rhymes with Italian Riviera.

Two girls came up to me and spoke in French. When I told them I spoke only English, they asked, in perfect English, about where to stamp their tickets. Then I remembered. Back in the Paris station I saw all these people rush up to a little orange machine right behind where Joan was sitting as we drank cafe noir. They stamped their tickets before they rushed off to the same train we got on. How come we hadn't stamped ours? Did these little multi-lingual girls know something we didn't? Would we have to go all the way back to Paris to get our tickets stamped?

We've found a charming hotel, the Chalet on Ouchy, which fits my idea of a perfect European hotel. Actually, this is more a house than a hotel, intimate and inviting. The woman who owns it seems like a cross between a kindly mother and a sophisticated businesswoman. She proudly declared herself to be 72 years old, yet she dresses in Bohemian or hippy fashion (choose your era), a profusion of skirts and paisley shawls. Her hair is wild and thick and curly like a young girl's. A talkative and happy woman who makes us feel at home. She tells us she was in a serious automobile accident in her 60's and was paralyzed for a while. But now she's totally recovered and physically active, a testament to the remarkable ability of even an old body to recuperate completely.

"The secret is to keep active," she says. It's good for me to hear, troubled as I am by sore knees and aching joints. Louisa May Alcott, when she took her Grand Tour, was also afflicted by rheumatic aches and pains. She refused to let them keep her from enjoying her tour, which lasted a whole year. Sometimes she, her sister and sister's friend would settle down in a hotel for weeks at a time. Talk about a leisurely trip. They stayed in Geneva for a week, at Vevay for a month, and in Rome for two months. Then onward to Munich, Cologne, Antwerp, and by boat to London. Much of their travel was by horse-drawn carriage. The Franco-Prussian war was raging, yet her spirits never flagged and she even began work on a new book, *Little Men*. On the boat home, a small pox epidemic broke out, but she was spared. So I should complain about sore knees?

JOAN

I love the quiet here. Even the voices of people going by beyond the hedges of the garden seem muted. A young couple walks by laughing and talking in French, of course, a language so lovely you could recite pork futures and it would still sound good.

That couple reminds me of Doug and me when we were young. Everything was a laugh, the days long and sunny, full of so much promise. And then it was sad. When did we start thinking the world wasn't ours? Ah well, that was long ago and regrets are futile. And we have less to regret than most divorced couples.

I haven't done a lot in my life that I'm really proud of but I have stayed loving friends with Doug and I am proud of that. We never made Dennis, our families or friends choose between us because we stayed loyal to each other. We met when we were sophomores in high school, have known each other nearly forty years. He's stayed a part of my family. And I got to keep Mona and Pat, his sisters, and all their children, my nieces and nephews.

I know I couldn't be any fonder of them if they were related to me by blood. What a funny expression that is. What's so important about blood? I think time is more important. Friends give each other time. Important time, trouble time, silly time, wasted time. Time spent together binds us together. Blood may be thicker than water. But time is thicker than blood.

Doug sang for both Mom and Dad's funerals. "I'm not sure I'll be able to do it without my voice cracking." he said when I asked him to sing. "After all, I love them too." But he sang beautifully. When Aunt Bernice was fatally ill, she asked Doug if he'd sing at her funeral. Bob kidded about being jealous that he wasn't chosen to sing and pretended that Doug, when asked, said, "Sure Bernice, what would you like to hear?" On the way down to her burial in Michigan, Bob and I took my Dad. My sister and Dennis rode with Doug. Bob decided that as he drove he would also practice singing IF YOU WANT TO BE A BADGER, the only song he knows all the way through. He said that he was planning to get up into the choir loft during the funeral mass, elbow Doug out of the way and start to sing.

"Won't my relatives think it's funny?" I said. "After all, the Wisconsin Fight Song is a strange choice for a funeral."

"I have that figured." Bob said. "I'm going to tell them it was Bernice's favorite song."

My father laughed so hard! And then he told everyone the story. One of my cousins came up to me after the funeral lunch and said, "I've only had one husband and he was a rat and left me with all the kids to raise. And you've had two good ones. Doesn't seem fair."

I had to agree.

PHEBE

I'm determined to keep active into old age, which no longer terrifies me. So many things I used to fear seem like chimeras now. Like getting up the courage to leave John at age 55. I did have friends who tried to warn me that it wouldn't be easy. "Hard to find another man at your age" is what one of my teaching colleagues said. When I ran into this same woman several months after I'd moved out, she greeted me brightly, "Have you started dating yet?"

Dating never did appeal to me even when I was young. The frantic preparations of the body so it would be appealing to the man, but not too appealing. The embarrassment of having to introduce my date to my father. He always asked, "And what does your father do, then?" followed by "And what church are you attending now, then?" and "What do you plan on doing after you graduate from Augsburg, then?"

Once this humiliation was hurdled, there was the lipstick problem. Since my father wouldn't let me wear makeup, I had to figure out a way to sneak on the lipstick without his knowing. I'd have the tube clutched in my hand and keep my face averted until I was safely in the car. Then, "Oh, just a minute. I forgot to put my lipstick on." The hurried adjustment of the rear view mirror, the leaning slightly toward the man as I reached forward to spread the color over my lips. "A carmine slash," as Joan used to call it. I claimed she'd stolen the phrase from some forties mystery writer, but she insisted it was her own. Lipstick was very important in those days. It was always a brilliant shade of red or coral. One looked extremely naked without it.

Once that little chore was out of the way, there was more tossing of the hair and final arranging of the dress so it wouldn't be wrinkled when the journey was over. Then the really hard part—finding something to talk about. Since I was totally ignorant of sports and totally uninterested, I could only hope, as did my father, that the young man would turn out to be interested in things I knew about—The Bible, Lutheran theology, Lutheran Free Church politics. Or my current favorite authors and poets, at that time T. S. Eliot and W. H. Auden. Once I found John, I knew I'd hit pay dirt.

His grandfather was a Lutheran minister and not only that, but in the same synod as my father. Unbelievable. He loved classical music and poetry and directed the choir at his church. He was able to give perfect answers to my father's questions and didn't even seem embarrassed by them. Furthermore, he himself was considering the ministry. Either that or going for his Ph.D., so he could be a college professor of history or philosophy.

We spent long hours walking around Minneapolis lakes, sitting on the floor in his parents' house where we were always welcome, reading aloud to each other from "For the Time Being" and "Prufrock." John identified with Prufrock and this scared me a bit. We went to a performance of "Murder in the Cathedral" at St. Mark's and we saw Elmer Rice's "Street Scene" at the Edyth Bush Little Theater, but we never went to movies until we were married because my father was opposed to them. Yes, John was a thoroughly suitable date, even by my father's standards.

MAY 24
JOAN

Sur La Plage—Lac Leman: Phebe has just announced, "It wouldn't matter what I'd brought along to wear on this trip, it would look like crap."

We have just had a non-stop, two-hour discussion of every outfit on every woman who walked by as we sat on stone benches along the lake. Phebe is possessed today by how inadequate our clothes are, how superior every other outfit we've seen today is, and just exactly what she would pack next time. She is furious that our fear made us pack such drab outfits in such a limited color scheme.

This is all on perhaps the most beautiful waterfront in Switzerland. Lac Leman is before us. Across the lake, the Alps rise snow-covered and serene on the distant shore. The colorful old town of Lausanne climbs the steep hills behind us. People are strolling along the lake and through the waterfront park which is filled with a profusion of flowers. Beautifully dressed people.

"I should have brought along huge, high heels. I could wear the same clothes but the heels would make all the difference," Phebe said. I tried to remind her that our serious laced-up comfort shoes were the direct result of her bad back before we left the States but she wasn't listening.

PHEBE

Yesterday I left Joan alone in the chalet while I went looking for Edward Gibbons' street and the cathedral where he converted back to Protestantism from Catholicism. After I'd walked only a couple of blocks, I missed the slight rise from sidewalk to street and fell splat forward onto the concrete. When I got up, I felt amazingly good, clearer somehow in my head than before. I'm like one of those old soap opera characters who used to get amnesia from a blow on the head. Then a second blow restored them to clarity about their previous lives and to the arms of their anguished lovers, who never lost faith they would return. Do I have some new clarity? To whom shall I return?

Later I sat in the cool cathedral to catch my breath It was quite an arduous hike to get there—first many long hills to climb and then the 217 steps from street level to the cathedral itself. All this climbing helps to prepare me for my Norway visit. I remember from 1950 how athletic my cousins were and I presume still are. They all skiied and hiked long distances into the mountains. The year my Aunt Johanna came from Norway to stay with us, she couldn't believe what a sedentary child I was, preferring to sit indoors reading, even on beautiful summer days. Once she made me hike the ten miles from Sacred Heart to the neighboring town of Granite Falls. I was only ten years old, but she assumed I could do it. I still brag to my kids about it.

Today Joan and I walked down to beautiful Lac Leman to contemplate the water and mountains, snow-covered in the distance. Unfortunately, I began observing other scenic wonders—the beautifully-dressed women, each one of whom had perfect traveling outfits. After all the many shopping trips Joan and I had devoted to our travel wardrobes, I still hadn't managed to do it right.

I saw a woman with beautiful high-heeled shoes, the kind I haven't worn for years. I made the mistake of saying to Joan, "Why didn't I bring any high-heeled shoes? Why oh why have I made myself into such a dumpy middle-aged woman by walking around in these low-heeled oxfords? They're just like the sensible lace-up shoes my stepmother made me wear in high school when all the other girls were wearing penny loafers. I'll bet all you Catholic girls wore penny loafers."

Joan pointed out being Catholic had nothing to do with wearing penny loafers and that I'd forgotten my bad back, the reason I'd bought the oxfords and decided to leave behind any dress shoes even with low heels.

But on to more intellectual matters. Apparently Edward Gibbons wasn't the only literary person to visit Lausanne. There's a street named after Charles Dickens and at the Hotel d' Angleterre we found this sign: "In this house June 1816 Lord Byron wrote 'The Prisoner of Chillon,' thereby adding one more deathless association to the already immortalized localities of this lake." Wish I knew more about Byron. Such a shame for an English major to have had the inadequate education I did. For one thing, going to a "good Christian college," as my father always referred to Augsburg, you can be sure I had only "good Christian" professors. When we read Byron in my British Lit. course, our professor skipped over him rather quickly because he wasn't a "real Christian." There was a lot of that in those days at Augsburg—judging who were "real" Christians. I remember a textbook we had for religion class, which I'm fond of telling Joan about. It was called *Christian Truths and Religious Delusions* and featured chapters with curious titles such as "Baptists: Some Truth, Some Error," "Seventh Day Adventists: Little Truth, Much Error," "Catholics: Much Truth, Much Error"

"Guess what the final chapter was?" I always ask Joan. She feigns not to know and I delight in spelling it out. "Lutherans: All Truth."

JOAN

When we climbed back up to the hotel, Madame was waiting for us. She tells us about an auto accident she had when she was 60. She is still driving at 72. "Accidents happen to people because they're living. If you have fear, if it stops you from doing what you wish to do, you miss life."

This sounds so much like my mother! Nothing stopped her. She was the first woman in her small town to go off to college, the first of six sisters to leave Michigan for higher-paying jobs on the Minnesota Iron Range. And I think she was the first woman on the Iron Range to demand equal pay for equal work. She asked the superintendent of schools why she wasn't being paid as much as a male teacher. He said it was because the man had six children. "Well," my mother replied, "are you paying us to teach or to breed?"

The women teachers got equal pay at the next meeting of the school board. And it didn't hurt my mother's career either. She was named assistant principal the following year.

She was physically unafraid too. At the age of 41, when most women of her generation were welcoming grandchildren, my mother had her first baby, my sister Pat. I was born a month shy of her 43rd birthday. She was a woman who always seemed to know what she wanted and who went after it.

How wretched for her to have a daughter like me, a woman for whom the term "ambivalent" could have been coined. It's all very well for feminists to keep on about how women should seize life by the throat and wrestle what they want from it. You can only start seizing and wrestling when you know what it is you've got by the throat.

Today young women talk confidently about their "Career Paths," a term which fills me with awe. It sounds like a perfectly-mowed, gently-inclined Path that leads up and out of sight, straight to Success. I imagine these new, smarter, tougher women climbing it as easily as mountain goats with just a stop or two along the Path to drop a Trophy Kid.

I've always had a rather tenuous grasp on career's throat. At St. Thomas the Apostle grade school we called careers "vocations." There were two big vocations for girls—Marriage or The Convent. I remember in 4th Grade, Sister Timothea asked us about our vocations and I cold-bloodedly thought of one that I was sure would guarantee me an "A" in Religion on my next report card. "I have decided to become a saint, Sister."

Although I'm sure I didn't fool Sister Timothea for a moment, she was too sweet to say more than a weak, "Really, Joan? I'm sure the other children and I will pray for you."

I felt the whole affair had gone rather well and tried it on my mother when I came home for lunch. There was just a second of silence and then she said coolly, "That's wonderful news. You can start by cleaning up your room, without complaining, when you get home from school. Saints never whine, you know." So it wasn't to be sainthood. Now here I am at fifty, still wondering about my vocation, my career, and less than ever a saint.

After talking to Madame, we turn in for a fairly early night, but Phebe doesn't rest easy because she had a long walk yesterday and a bad fall on her trip to the cathedral and is aching, bruised, and full of scrapes. She woke up moaning about 2 am. Luckily we had some brioches to munch on. There's always a little something in our ever-present plastic sacks. We laughed about the crumbs we were leaving in beds all over Europe and soon fell back asleep.

PHEBE

I want to come back to Lausanne and I will "if the Lord tarries," as my father used to say. He believed in the Rapture, the Second Coming of Jesus. He might arrive at any moment so we must always be ready. "Do nothing you would not want to be doing when Jesus comes." Now that my father's dead, I've come to love all his old sayings, although when he was alive, I was annoyed by them. I feared and resented him for so long, but I'm learning to accept him at last. I hope he knows I did love him, even though we never said "I love you" to each other.

I remember the only time he was ever in a hospital. How astonished I was to see him sitting on the edge of the bed in his short hospital gown. Didn't the nurses know my father never wore anything in public except a black suit with vest, white shirt, tie and jacket, even while mowing his lawn? He didn't want members of his congregation to see him in casual clothes. Might give them a bad impression of ministers. Wasn't dignified.

Before I left that night I decided to take a big risk and hug him goodbye.

Hugging was unheard of in our family. We were Norwegian, proud of never showing our emotions. I tentatively put my arms around him. He seemed so frail, so vulnerable in his pitiful gown. Was this the father I'd been afraid of all my life? But his arms remained stiffly at his sides. "Oh Phebe," he said. "You shouldn't."

7. ON THE ITALIAN RIVIERA
Time out from the Grand Tour

MAY 25

JOAN

U p and out on the Lausanne Metro. It's fast, cheap and it delivers us right to the railroad station in plenty of time to catch our train for the Italian Riviera. Transportation in Europe is so well planned. There are subways and buses to the train stations, trains to the airports and seaports, and the transport companies consider each other so that schedules coincide and travel is easy.

We're going to the seashore for a couple of days before Rome. This mini-vacation was something we decided we would need when planning the trip. Traveling is hard work and we are determined to make our Grand Tour leisurely, unhurried, peaceful.

This morning our train is late, first late train we've had. Oh well, when it did come it was wonderful. Our private compartment has two window seats, glass doors to the corridor, red plush seats and purple curtains. It's a good thing we both have window seats this morning as the scenery is superb. First the train swoops down one side of Lac Leman. Then it burrows right through the Alps in tunnel after tunnel. As we come out for air here and there, rushing walls and curtains of water seem close enough to touch, coming straight down from the tops of the mountains above us. If you had the nerve, you could open a window and wash your hair right from the train.

We whiz through one beautiful town after the next—Montreaux, Sion, Brig and the first town in Italy, Domodossolo. We travel by Lake Laverno with its incredible resort towns. Stressa seems like a good town from which to start a visit to this coast.

As we near Milano, we return to our favorite conversation—the paucity of our wardrobes, looks, education and cultural level as compared with European women we've seen. We solemnly agree to go to a weight class as soon as we get home. We will throw out all our discount store clothes and buy one or two perfect outfits each. Make sure we really care for our body and skin. Learn to speak at least three languages. Get a grip on culture. Music. Art. Architecture. History. Foreign literature. But first, off comes the weight. And when we return we will have transformed ourselves into two perfect European women.

"Ah, la bella Italia," Phebe has just said. It's her first attempt at the Italian language and her last. I thought I had convinced her that it was her job to look through our phrase books and attempt to speak Italian because I had taken care of us from Belgium on with my high school French. She refuses, saying, "I'm not trying Italian. I'll speak English and force them to understand me. After all, I'm the customer."

It was so hot changing trains in Milan and the station was so huge. We had a long, long walk from one train to another. But what a wonderful station. We bought a complete picnic lunch at food stands, including crusty loaves of freshly-baked bread. It also had dozens of baggage handlers, looking very romantic in long blue coats and pulling wooden carts. All talking a mile a minute.

In Genoa I've come to my own people in the land of the wash. Everyone has laundry hanging out and in the crowded downtown district there are lines running between buildings, heavy with clothes. I wonder if there are laundry competitions? You can see how many clothes your neighbors have and how often they change their sheets.

We just crossed the Tiber, river of childhood geography lessons. The feeling here is dreamlike, familiar. Coming home to Italy. There are acres and acres of rice paddies, a surprise. Under water, you can see the shoots of rice beginning, a tender, pale green. How do they irrigate them? It seems so dry here. In 1½ hours we'll go from the industrial north to the Mediterranean. We're busily reading tour books, deciding where to stay tonight on the Cinque Terra, five ancient and tiny towns right on the sea. The name means five earths in Italian, and a friend of mine told me she thinks these towns must be the most beautiful places on earth.

We change trains again in Genoa and it's a scene straight out of a comic Italian opera. They couldn't make up their minds what binario (platform) the train to La Spezia and the Cinque Terra would leave from. So they kept changing the number. As each new number was called, the entire platform of people, as one, would go down the flight of stairs, under the tracks and then hurry up the stairs of the new binario. This happened three or four times, a horde of people disappearing and popping up out of the ground again like one large rabbit.

We did get a local out of Genoa almost as soon as we had arrived, and it is full, full to the brim with young Italians in beach gear talking, talking with extravagant gestures, and never seeming to listen. The train ride along the sea is bella, bella. It stops at every town, every one and takes 2¼ hours to go the little distance from Genoa to Monterosso where we're getting off.

And the towns! All right on the Meditarranean, every one a jewel of beauty—Sestri Levante, Rapallo, Civa, Levanto. I could get off this train anywhere and settle down. I'd look for a local English Social Club and enroll in Italian language classes. I wonder what it would be like to live somewhere you didn't know a soul and have to rely totally on yourself for company. I suppose I'll never know if I have the inner resources to do such a thing. I don't suppose I do. It sounds terribly lonely.

Freud supposedly asked, "What do women want, anyway?" which is one of the reasons I don't trust psychiatry. The answer is so simple. We want to connect. I think women feel like lamps that never get plugged in. Or that we're leaving our message to the world on an answering machine that never gets played back.

Bob and I spent hours on long-distance telephone calls late at night when we were dating. We explored our thoughts, hopes, fears, plans for the future, and every little nuance of our feelings for one another. Finally I felt connected. Months after we were married, Bob confessed that he had been worried. "You went from one subject to another," he said. "You seemed to want to talk about everything. I didn't say anything then, but I thought you were probably drinking too much."

PHEBE

We're in Heidi country now. How I loved that book by Johanna Spyri. I can still see the cover picture of Heidi and her grandfather making their way up the mountain, where she was to live after her mother died. I was sent to live with my grandparents in Duluth and so felt Heidi was a kindred spirit. My grandfather wasn't as gruff as Heidi's. We went everywhere together. I remember often walking down to Bridgeman-Russell's to buy triple dip ice cream cones for a nickel. Then we'd climb back up the four hilly blocks to our house. The ice cream was almost as good as the melted cheese and toasted bread Heidi's grandfather made for her.

One day, my grandfather walked me to the public library, an imposing stone building with strange floors made out of glass blocks. How magical to walk upon glass! Once I knew the way, I went often to the library by myself. It was a place of refuge, a place where I could lose myself in stories that took me away from the great tragedy of my life—that my mother had left me forever. I took five books home, all I was allowed at one time. Then I'd settle in with my cache on the second-floor porch, which looked out over Lake Superior. Of all the characters in all the books I read that year, Heidi, motherless child of another time and country, was my dearest companion.

My grandmother usually stayed home, sunk in sadness over the death of her only daughter. It must have been hard for her to have me there, a constant reminder of what she'd lost. But maybe I was a comfort to her, too.

We're in Italy. We've passed through the towns of Verazzo and Stresa and now we're in Domodossola. I love

writing these Italian names and pronouncing them aloud in a soft voice to myself when no one can hear to correct me. Guess I'll get out my phrase book and start learning a few useful Italian words. HELP! for instance. You ought to know how to say HELP! in any language.

Time to figure out Italian money. There are 14.4 lira to the penny, so 1000 lira equals 70 cents. Fifty dollars a day means 72,000 lira. Joan wakes up and I say, "Don't these gorgeous bills make American money look sick? Don't you think we need to jazz up our American bills? Look how their money has pictures of Michelangelo and other artists and writers, not just politicians. And all in full color!" She agrees, then adds, "I'm surprised you noticed. Money usually goes through your hands so fast you hardly have time to see the color or the size, not to mention its aesthetic qualities."

MAY 26

JOAN
(SUPRA SPIAGGIA: ON THE BEACH)

There's a dog here this morning who looks just like Arnold, which gives me a pang. Arnold, my Three-Legged Dog, is a sorry, shopworn fifteen this year. He lost one leg to a fox trap and all but six teeth to a cow he chased and unfortunately caught. His hair is long and matted and he's torn great clumps of it out with his few remaining teeth. When we walk, he wheezes, runs out of breath at the corner and sometimes when he lifts a leg, he falls right over. Arnold is an Unknown Quanity, a rarity in our neighborhood where pets have better bloodlines than the Queen of England. When someone asks me what breed Arnold is, I tell them he's a pure-blooded Parts-Missing Dog. And I miss him a lot this morning. How is he and how is old snarl-puss Delilah, the World's Oldest Living Cat?

But I digress. It's easy to do, sitting at a little yellow-clothed table next to flowering oleanders and about ten feet from the turquoise blue Mediterranean. Mother Sea. There isn't a cloud in the sky, and the street scene is so much fun to watch and listen to. These people are alive and they love it.

We arrived here so hot and tired and I was a little scared too. It was 5:30 pm, we had no room and it looked as though half of Italy was in Monterosso. We walked along the sea less than two blocks from the train station and stopped at the Hotel Cerona, the one a man at the station told Phebe we'd like, after she went into her sleeping act in mime. Then we had a wonderful, frustrating conversation at the desk with a man who obviously owned the hotel.

"I have no English, no English," he screamed in anguish, pounding his forehead and rocking his head down towards the counter. But he did speak French about as well as I do and so we limped slowly together towards understanding.

It turns out that the Cerona is a hotel pensione with two meals included in the price of the room, a petit dejeuner from 8-9:30 am and dinner at 7:45 pm. The price per person, per day is 45,000 lire so our total bill, he tells us tragically, the tears almost spilling, will be

270,000 lire. Sounded way beyond our resources so I whipped out my handy converter and what to our eyes did appear but $30 a day per person for a room and two meals. Magnifico. Yet we imagined that for this low price the room would be terrible.

Wrong. It's perfect. I'll try to describe it exactly so that I will always remember it. Tall windows covered with long, green shutters opening to a balcony that overlooks the main curve of the beach. The hotel is just about in the middle of a circle of beach that embraces the town of Monterosso. There's a sink and douche behind a privacy screen of carved wood and net. A wooden cupboard for our clothes. Two beds with one headboard, small bedside tables with reading lamps. A writing desk. The overhead light hangs from a ceiling which is at least 20 feet away. The walls are apple green on the bottom with white tops. The floor is terrazzo with an inlaid pattern in marble that forms a cloverleaf at every corner.

The whole room shimmers with light when the shutters are open, a dancing light reflected from the sea below. When the shutters are closed, the room is bathed in a sea-green light, like being under water. The sound of the sea, the surf, is constant. Standing out on the balcony, the view left is towards town and the winding walking path through the hills to Vernazza. To the right is Il Gigante, an enormous Hercules carved out of the rock. Straight ahead is the incredible blue of the Mediterranean. There's a boy asleep on the beach in a sleeping bag. Fishing boats, in colored waves, are coming in from sea.

We're the only Americans in the dining room tonight. Dinner starts with a pasta course, then a veal dish, then creme caramel. All really good. I can't believe we've found this perfect place or that we can afford it. We've landed on our feet in Italy, hurrah.

PHEBE
(MONTEROSSO)

We arrived last night and found a hotel, thanks to my ingenuity. Joan cruelly put me in charge of Italian, of making all requests for rooms and meals and bathrooms in Italy. Said it would be good for me to get a little practice being assertive. Furthermore, she pointed out, I should be willing to try a little Italian, since I keep talking about how I had Latin in high school. "They're both Romance languages, you know. Surely some words are similar." Whereupon she handed me her book, *Italian for Travelers*, with everything phonetically spelled out.

So I gamely went up to the information counter in the train station and mimed the need for sleep. I must say I did it quite grandly and gracefully, with excessive gestures and facial expressions. I, who have always hated mimes, am now forced to use this miserable method to find a place to lay my head.

We were directed, with lots of pointing, to a hotel. When we still seemed confused, the man came right out from behind his counter and pointed us down the street in the right direction to this great hotel right on the beach, the Cerona. We're in paradise. The building is that creamy stucco I love and has white cement balconies, solid as the Rock of Ages. Perhaps that's a blasphemous reference. "Solid as the Rock of Gibraltar" is what I actually said to Joan when she expressed fear that perhaps the balcony off our room might not hold both our weights. "Nonsense," I said. "Of course it will." Then I added with my relentless and somewhat devilish devotion to truth, "But you do often read of whole Italian wedding parties on balconies plunging to their deaths." Joan was unabashed. "Why always wedding parties?" she asked, having read the same news stories. "Why not christening parties or funeral gatherings, whole wakes maybe."

I would have slept the whole night through in my comfortable bed had I not been awakened at 2 am by loud singing. When I got up and looked down, I saw a group of teen-age girls below our balcony. "My Darling Clementine" and "Are You Sleeping, Brother John?" sung in English with French accents were their entire repertoire, and they sang both songs loudly many times. Why did they choose to serenade us? Had they been misinformed and told that two darling American male students were staying in our room?

We've finished our breakfast of hard rolls, butter,

marmalade, and cappuccino in the dining room of our hotel, taken our writing materials and moved out to the tables on the sidewalk. Joan is writing her 18th postcard to Bob. I believe she numbers them, else how did she know to tell me that? I have this nagging feeling I should be writing post cards, but I'd rather sit and gaze out at the Mediterranean.

A garbage truck passes by, inscribed: "Comune de Monterosso." Seems so much classier than any sign I've ever seen on a garbage truck back in St. Paul. If I'm so enthralled by the Italian language, why didn't I give more serious attention to learning it before I left home? Or now that I'm here, why don't I try harder to speak out a few harmless phrases that can't possibly be misinterpreted? I feel inspired right now to exclaim aloud, "Bella Italia!" Did I spell it right? Who cares. It's only in my journal. But as Virginia Woolf once wrote, "It's important to look good, even to yourself." It's the old demon fear, I guess, that keeps me silent. Fear of my pronunciation being laughed at, although for some reason I'm not quite as afraid of trying Italian as French. Italian seems more natural and forgiving than French. And easier, perhaps, because of my high school Latin, which I'm always reminding Joan of. I may have been Lutheran and had to go to public schools, but I knew my Latin.

I'm intrigued by the people passing by. I try to get Joan to stop writing postcards and talk to me. "Joan," I say, "Dorothy Lamour just walked by." (I thought that would get her attention.) "Can't be," she answers, without looking up. "She's dead." "She is not," I say. "I know I read an article about her before I left Monte." "Must have been about someone else. I know she's dead."

Then we degenerate into "Is too dead!" "Is not dead!" "Is too!" "Is not!" Joan breaks the impasse by wondering how I'd recognize Dorothy Lamour, anyway, since I had such a movie-deprived childhood. "Well, then, maybe it wasn't Dorothy Lamour," I say. "Maybe it was Lana Turner." I tell her I had seen one movie, "Somewhere I'll Find You," starring Clark Gable and Lana Turner, while I was still living in my father's house. My high school boyfriend had tricked me into getting on the streetcar with him one Sunday afternoon, saying we were going to Como Park. Actually, he planned to get me into a movie theatre, knowing full well I was forbidden to go. My father trusted me with this boy because, after all, he did go to our church and thus was considered a safe bet.

Back to Dorothy Lamour. To tell you the truth, the woman I'd seen was not wearing a sarong, but had tied a large sheer India-print scarf around her swim suit in sarong-fashion. But I'm certainly not going to admit that to Joan!

MAY 27

JOAN
(THE CINQUE TERRE)

This morning we visited the tourist bureau to learn the best way to see the other four towns. After a long walk through the village, we went to the post office, bought some cards and letter paper. The town is ancient and colorful, long and skinny, and all on the sea. Behind it are hills and hills, full of grape vines. The Cinque Terre is famous for its wine. We bought some food and had a picnic on a bench overlooking the sea, near some bunkers left over from World War II.

After a relaxing morning, we had a nice siesta in the afternoon. We wanted to see the other towns but what's the rush? Now we're awake and up and out for Vernazza. We're taking the Locale, a little local train that runs happily up and down the seashore, taking passengers from one beauty to the next.

No one asks to see our Eurail Passes. They haven't since we entered Italy. No one ever seems to come through the trains asking for tickets. I feel the whole country must be riding trains for free.

Vernazza tumbles down the hills and ends on a small crescent beach. It's so beautiful it makes my eyes fill with tears. We're in a cafe right in the middle of the beach, under overlapping umbrellas in orange and teal and red and gold. Bellissima! We've been through Corniglia and Manarola, long hard climbs from the stations down to the towns. We decide to train down to the last town of the Cinque Terra and thus see them all. It's Riomaggiore and it is incredible.

Fishing boats in a tumble everywhere on the beach. And the colors. How I wish I could paint. Ochre. Bright blue. Terra cotta. Light pink. All jumbled together, the colors on some boats new, some worn nearly off. The buildings are very old and glow with color, from palest apricot to a warm brownish pink. All work together to form an incredible—there's that word again—whole. These towns could make one run out of adjectives, I tell Phebe, and it's the pure truth.

On the train back to Monterosso, a 15-minute ride from Riomaggiore, we feel as though we're coming home. Quite a different feeling from our arrival. This mini-vacation has been wonderful for both of us, we agree.

PHEBE
(MONTEROSSO)

We've taken the local train to come to the second in the chain of five little villages that make up the Cinque Terre. Now we're sitting on a cement ledge, the rocky harbor at our feet. Many boats moored here, jumbled together in a picturesque mess of masts and flags. Pink and orange and pale yellow stucco houses rise behind us against the hills, which are covered with terraced rows of grapes, the vines looped over an intricate network of stakes, rickety and home-made looking but marvelously picturesque.

I have the odd sensation of being at home in these exotic surroundings. Have I lived a former life here? Rather, I think it's because of pictures I've seen in travel magazines, but also because several of my favorite houses in Sacred Heart were Mediterranean in feeling and style. My friend whose father owned the biggest store in town, lived in a house on what we called "Silk Stocking Street." Her house was pale pink stucco, large and luxurious, and had a sunken living room, plus many other features I think of as Mediterranean, like walls of swirling patterned plaster. Elaborate wrought iron candle sconces on the walls. Fireplaces, even in the bedrooms, were set into arches, which made them seem grotto-like.

We are reading in our guidebooks about some sight that is "beautiful beyond belief." Joan says, "Why should we bother seeing it, since we're not going to believe it anyway?" That makes me laugh and then barely a few beats later, she says, gazing out at some women passing by, whom we presume to be locals, "The women our age in this town are very old." That gets us both to laughing.

We're in the little town of Vernazza, another jewel in the Cinque Terre crown.

Writing "jewel" makes me think of an old Sunday School hymn. It always chilled my heart. Whenever we sang it, I was certain I'd have to say "No" were I to give a response to its musical question: "Will there be any jewels, any jewels in my crown?/ When in heaven my burden I lay down?/ When I wake with the blest, in the mansions of rest/ Will there be any jewels in my crown?"

Strange how my mind offers up the words of that hymn as I sit writing in the bright Mediterranean sunshine. Our Sunday School teacher, Mrs. Vigstad, older than my grandmother, with several hairs bristling on her several chins, would ask us sternly, "What jewels are you getting ready for your crowns, children?" Turns out they were things like obeying your mother and father, being kind to others, even brothers and sisters, offering to run errands for neighbors, obeying your teachers, and of course, listening to your minister when he preached the sermon. Hard for me since my father was my minister. Oh yes, reading the Bible every day counted, too, and saying your prayers before you went to sleep, even if it was "Now I lay me down to sleep," with its grim possibility that you, a mere child, might die before dawn.

Of course, my father mandated family devotions, so I suppose I couldn't count them as my jewels. Each day my father would take out the King James Bible after breakfast and supper to read aloud excruciatingly long passages, then expound on them endlessly, and finally conclude with a rambling prayer that started with requests for our family's spiritual health and then continued to our relatives in Norway and Sweden, as well as to the millions of heathen, including Roman Catholics.

Joan has just said she wants to take my picture. I protest, saying I don't want my picture taken with this scarf wound tightly around my head. It's the one I bought in Brussels and it certainly has come in handy. This morning when I realized my hair was impossible, I quickly pressed the scarf into service, wrapping it like a turban around my head, the way we used to in the 1940's. Something Dorothy Lamour would have done, or would do, since I'm sure she's still alive. Joan said the scarf made me look like an Italian peasant and now she wants to take my picture underneath a poster that features a hammer and sickle. Since I was once spat upon during a peace demonstration in the 1960s and called a "commie bitch," I decide a picture would be appropriate, after all.

The spitting took place during my very first peace walk in 1958 when Erik was our only child. Those were the glorious days when I never gave a thought to any other career beyond that of wife and mother. I wasn't very political, either, but we had Quaker friends who invited us on the peace walk. Afterwards, we would play tennis and have a picnic. We piled Erik and the stroller into our Morris Minor, along with tennis rackets and picnic lunch. Demonstration in the morning. Fun in the afternoon. Sounded perfect to me.

Little did I dream an ugly crowd would gather along the peaceful avenue. As I was pushing the stroller past my favorite department store, it happened. An ordinary-looking man, wearing a suit and carrying a brief case, yelled at me, called me a "Commie bitch." I wouldn't have been certain he meant me, except he followed this name-calling with a well-directed shot of spittle that landed squarely on my hand as I wheeled Erik along.

That was the inauspicious beginning to my long involvement in the peace and civil rights movement. I was especially drawn to fund-raising activities that combined my homemaking skills with good causes. For years I baked up to three dozen loaves of bread every week on the old restaurant-size gas range we inherited when we bought our house. Joan was my best marketing agent. She took orders from her advertising friends. The amount of money I made was small, but I donated it all to my peace and justice organizations. Being a wife and homemaker seemed truly worthwhile in those days. It meant having time to volunteer my talents to all sorts of worthy causes from PTA to church to League of Women Voters to the Democratic party. It never occurred to me I needed a job to feel fulfilled, because I thought I had a vocation.

JOAN

I'm sleeping like a log on this trip, and I've spent quite a lot of time wondering why, when the places are always strange and we've moved so frequently. The beds have been all over the lot too—soft, hard, big, small.

I worried about sleeping over here because I slept so poorly in Switzerland on that ski trip with Bob and our friends. I think it's because we're getting so much exercise walking and also because I'm not nervous. On vacations with Bob I always have this fluttery feeling that I'm letting him down, especially when we're with other people who are as good as he is at whatever dangerous and physical thing we're doing at the time. I'm usually scared and trying not to show it. But I guess I do show it because he has told me often I'm "ruining" trips for him and others with my fear. I remember lying awake in Engelbert, heart pounding, mouth dry, wondering if I should take lessons and brave the fearsome Alps or tell the others I just wouldn't ski.

It's strange how being so far away from Bob and home can make me see things about our relationship so clearly. For instance, I'm sure now that it would have been much better to simply say firmly and quietly, "I'm not skiing the Alps. They terrify me. I'll sit in the hotel and read or go for long walks up and down the mountains on the perfectly shoveled Swiss paths."

This probably would have been just fine with Bob. He's not a monster of cruelty, after all, just someone who loves danger and likes to have me along while he's engaging in it. What angers him is my pretending to go along with the day's plan until retching and sniveling, I find myself at the top of an impossible mountain with no way down but on my skis or strapped onto a Ski Patrol toboggan.

Lordy, lordy this whole man-woman thing is such a mystery. I was just getting really good at dating when I got married and all the rules changed. Then I was wonderful, I thought, at being married just when I got the news that I was being divorced. About two minutes after I was finally comfortable being single, I got married again. And there's a whole new set of rules to learn for a second marriage.

Oh the perversity. You want someone a lot, he doesn't want you. Lose interest? He's all over you like fog. It's never equal, never. Even a good relationship is more like a teeter-totter with first one, then the other getting the emotional upper seat.

Funny thoughts sitting here in the beautiful cool of early evening on the blue, blue sea. I'm alone at a table in front of our yellow and white hotel. Phebe has gone up, it's 7:05 pm and dinner will be in 40 minutes. I'd better wash the beach and sand off my feet. I love it here so.

8. IN THE ETERNAL CITY
We get ourselves to a nunnery

MAY 28

PHEBE
(TRAIN TO ROME)

Here we are, on another slow train going from Monterosso to Rome. This morning we had our last look at the Mediterranean from the balcony of the Hotel Cerona. Below us, we could see a tourist sitting at one of the tables, already at work on his day's quota of postcards. I've fallen rather shamefully behind on my cards, while Joan has each day "stuck to task," as we used to say in the education business.

Why do I feel I have to keep up with her? There's no one who's really expecting to hear from me, the way Bob expects to hear from her. Once when a friend and I were commiserating over our divorces, she told me how bad she'd felt when her former husband went off on a trip without her to see mutual friends. She couldn't even call to find out if he'd made it safely. "It seemed to me then the whole world was on a buddy system, except me," she said.

Yet even while I realize it's a couple's world, I'm feeling less and less tied to being married. Leah said to me just before I left, "Mom, I think you're happier now than you were those last years you were married to dad. In fact, both of you seem happier now, if you want to know what I think." That's what I find hard to accept, that he's probably happier, too, out of the marriage. I'd like to think he's suffering without me, that he desperately wants me back. But why? Would I want to go back? Do I just like the idea of being married, not the actuality?

JOAN

We were told to take only a yellow cab when arriving in Rome. The train stations and airports are dense with young men speaking fairly good English who own their own purple, pink, black, white or blue cabs. Do not get into one. You will get out again but most of your lire will be gone. The yellow cabs are said to be licensed by the government and charge consistent, albeit enormous, amounts.

Our young brigand met us as we got off the train from the Cinque Terre, grabbed Phebe's bag and threw it into his off-white cab. We were then his prisoners. He insisted he knew the way to Villa Rosa, a convent where we are to stay for our days in and around Rome. He probably did know where it was, but this didn't stop him from driving us around for an hour, stopping every block to ask a pedestrian if he or she had ever heard of the Villa Rosa.

When we arrived at the convent, our cabbie lost his English completely and started speaking very fast and very threateningly in Italian. We did understand that he felt we owed him a great deal of money. Furious, I got out of the cab and rang the bell hanging on the gates of Villa Rosa to get some help from the nuns inside. Phebe, left alone, realized that all of our luggage was in the trunk of the robber cab and that if we both jumped out, he might take off with all of our belongings, including our unspent traveler's checks.

Terrified, Phebe had whipped out her billfold and was pelting the cabbie with money when I returned. He grabbed $30 and wouldn't give it back no matter how I shouted. He threw our bags in the street and sped off just as Sister Gabrielle came to our rescue.

She led us through the wooden door in the thick, outer walls of Villa Rosa, into the cool and calm of the convent yard. The yard was filled with the sweet, first roses of spring and purple banks of clematis. Inside the front hall, I almost wept when I smelled that mixture of beeswax and, very faintly, incense, the smell of every convent, every cloister, and every Catholic school I had ever been in. To me, it is the smell of order, serenity, peace. I was at home in Rome.

EVENING: This convent is heaven. Tall, yellow stucco with wooden shuttered windows and a high yellow wall around the entire yard. Inside, there are statues, holy pictures and flickering votive lights everywhere. Outside, a profusion of roses and other flowers. Hence the name I suppose. Our room is huge, three twin beds, a high, high ceiling with plaster frescos, a washstand and lots of cupboards and closets. The enormous marble bath is right next door.

I love the nuns too. They're Dominicans from Ireland and throughout the school year act as hosts for college students visiting Rome from Dominican colleges all over the world. They're talkative, friendly, down-to-earth, so Irish. Sister Gabrielle is fast, positive, witty, divine.

Bitter disappointment here. Just one very short letter from Bob and I had expected six. His explanation is convoluted and strange. What I think he is saying is that he has sent six letters and shot-gunned them all over Europe. I remember telling him Rome was one of three stops where I could be assured of getting mail. I suppose he thought of a better way, he usually does. Never mind if his way doesn't work, it is creative. Somehow, though, tonight I can't stand it.

Tired, hot, horribly dirty and very homesick, it hurts me that he has done this. I go on about it so long that Phebe snaps at me. A poor start for Rome. A husband who isn't writing to me and a friend who's mad at me. I feel alone in Rome, a city so vast and old that it makes me feel small and momentary which of course I am. But who likes feeling that vulnerable?

The nuns just knew that we would want to see the Pope so they have applied for tickets for us tomorrow. They consider it a treat beyond compare. I wonder what Phebe, daughter of a Lutheran minister who preached often about Papacy wrongs, is thinking.

PHEBE

We're at the Villa Rosa, where wonderful Sister Gabrielle greeted us. We called her Mother Gabrielle at first but she corrected us, saying in her no-nonsense, Irish-inflected English, "Oh no. We're all sisters here." She showed us to our room and I fell in love with it. Windows, almost floor to ceiling, are framed with beautiful heavy wood and opened with highly polished big brass knobs. We look out on the rooftops of Rome, all tangled together in a rich exuberance of colors, textures, architectural styles.

Three narrow single beds. Who shall sleep in the third one? "The unseen listener to every conversation, of course," I say to Joan. "Or the unseen sleeper in every empty bed—Jesus himself." She said I made her nervous talking about sacred things like that. "Why do you Lutherans have to get sex into everything?" "Why, Joan," I say, "I wasn't thinking of sex. Beds don't necessarily represent sex to me."

The old yearning to be Catholic has come upon me here again. I first felt it in childhood when my best friend was Catholic. Her mother was Catholic, but her father wasn't. My father told us that non-Catholics who married a Catholic had to sign an agreement to raise all the children Catholic. He thought that was horrible, but I didn't. The Catholic religion, filled with mystery and glamour, seemed much more interesting than mine.

Some of the mystery has disappeared because of all the talking Joan and I do about our religions. Joan has never understood all the restrictions I lived with, like not being able to go to movies or play cards. Joan would love to teach me to play bridge, is sure I could learn, but I steadfastly refuse. Bridge is not only one of the pleasures of her life, but her key to living well into old age. She read an article that claimed bridge and crossword puzzles were the two best activities to keep your mind alert as you age. I don't work crossword puzzles, either. Early on, I relinquished that pastime to John. I often say to Joan, "Maybe you can teach him to play bridge when the two of you come to visit me, wasting away in the nursing home, mumbling all the old poetry I memorized in grade school."

"What makes you think John will visit you in the nursing home?" she always asks. Funny, but I just know that's something he'd do. I can count on it.

MAY 29

JOAN

Up and out early at the Villa Rosa. The breakfast room had many other guests, all from Ireland. Such a grand clatter of soft Irish voices this morning. One of the guests from Dungarven, Ireland, kept me reaching for my journal. She described a friend who showed great coolness and courage during an emergency as "she never lost a feather." Explaining her late start (7 am!), she said she had been out late the night before and "this morning I'm all panned out." Her still-sleeping husband and son were explained by "they're mucking in this morning."

Phebe and I decided to plunge right into public transportation. We got some help from the nuns and it turns out to be fairly easy. Also we'll save lots of money, meet real Europeans and learn the city better. Whizzing through a foreign city in a cab is for Americans with more cash than curiosity, more timidity than time, we decided.

Rome is difficult. But after we learn some simple things, I think we'll be able to bus everywhere we want to go. First, the location of the TERMINI, the square and depot from which all buses flow in Rome. Here we made friends with the men in the information kiosk and bought a week-long pass for 10,000 lire. It's good on any bus and allows us unlimited travel in the city and out to the suburbs.

We also memorized the number of the buses that stop within a block of our convent home. If we can't figure out on the map how to get somewhere or find a passenger who speaks enough English to explain it to us, we'll just ride the bus down to the Termini and start and end our day's adventures from there.

Later in St. Peter's Square, we're waiting for the Pope to come in. Looking around, I can't believe it. There are thousands, thousands of people here already and thousands more pouring in from every side. It's hot, hot, there's a sea of open umbrellas and it's only 9 am.

A band is playing hymns, many delegations are carrying or dragging things, statues and crosses, which embarrasses me and then I am ashamed of the embarrassment. Perhaps this is what worship should be. It's religious ceremony, circus, parade, a babbling United Nations of languages. Looking out at the arms of the square, the colonnades are topped with statues, perfectly arranged, so pleasing to the eye. They're working on the front of the Basilica. It's draped in scaffolding like half the buildings in Europe.

I can't believe I'm here, part of it, united with my fellow Catholics. I've always known that catholic means universal but today, for the first time, I truly understand it.

I take out Mom's rosary that I always keep with me since she died. She got it when she graduated from college, had it blessed when she had a semi-private audience with the Pope when she was here as a young school teacher in the 1920's. The sight of it, the thought of her so fresh, so eager makes me sad.

The Pope arrives without fanfare. He seems a very simple man, little, tired, and round-shouldered in the midst of all this panoply of Mother Church. He's completely in the open, at the mercy of any madman, first as he rides around the square on a high seat on the back of a small, white Jeep and now as he sits on the altar, on a high dais so that everyone can see. It cannot be safe, it's making me so nervous.

He speaks in Italian, Polish, English, Spanish, German and a language I don't recognize. His English is surprisingly good, his last words "in the struggle between good and evil, the last word will always belong to love."

PHEBE

Right now we're in St. Peter's Square, waiting for the Pope to arrive. Trumpets and other horned instruments are playing a LUTHERAN hymn:

> *Praise to the Lord, the Almighty, the King of Creation!*
> *Oh, my soul praise Him, for He is my health and salvation!*
> *All ye who hear, now to His temple draw near.*
> *Join me in glad adoration!*

Surely this hymn is a sign that the two shall soon be one. We Lutherans shall soon return to the Mother Church. Or maybe they'll come over to us.

An intense Italian sun pounds down on our heads. Thousands have swarmed in to see and hear His Holiness. A group of weary pilgrims arrives, dragging an enormous cross. They're from Mexico, according to their banners. Joan tells me not to look. "This is the sort of thing that makes me embarrassed to be a Catholic," she says. "This kind of excess. Drives me crazy." But I love it, find it intriguing and thrilling and even moving.

Everybody's wearing hats. Joan's and mine have been created out of our Rome maps, folded the way I used to fold newspaper hats for the kids' birthday parties. I also brought my umbrella to give us further shade, even though Joan thought I was nuts to drag it along. "Funny how you refused to bring an umbrella in Amsterdam when it was raining, but now you've brought one and have opened it in full sunshine!"

We waited for the Pope two hours. Finally he arrived in a white Jeep, an inappropriate vehicle for His Holiness, I thought. He didn't seem to mind, stood up to wave and smile as he was driven around through the crowd. Then he addressed us in French, Italian, German, and Polish. "Good reason I could never be Pope," I said to Joan. "I'd have to be multilingual." She pointed out several more important obstacles. "Perhaps you've forgotten, Phebe, that you are a woman, a layperson, and worst of all, a Lutheran!"

Now he's speaking in English. I'm trying to copy every word: "I want to speak today about the relationship between God's providence and human freedom. We ask if God is present, how is it possible for people to do evil? God's respect for our freedom is so great he allows us to sin, even though sin stands in direct opposition to what God wants. This shows how much God wishes us to be free. But God has foreseen for us a way of making up for sin—a way of redemption. In the struggle between good and evil, the last word belongs to love. I greet all English-speaking pilgrims and wish them well. May God bless you and your families."

Simple words but thrilling to hear from the very mouth of the Pope himself. Never mind all the times I heard my father preach against the papacy and sow seeds of distrust and anti-Catholicism in his sermons. Now I'm hoping for the unity of the One True Church.

MAY 30

JOAN

Today we wandered the little squares and streets of Rome and this evening went to the Piazza Navona, an old and wonderful carnival of a place with ancient churches, acres of open-air cafes and the fabulous fountain of Four Rivers by Bernini. We had dinner and then a scary walk in twisty, dark Roman streets and a bus ride with leering men. The town is full of anti-American graffitti because of the bombing of Libya—"Yankee Assassini!" "Yank Go Home", "Reagan Assassini!" to mention the ones I understood.

It's hard to feel hated, even when it's this impersonal, all-you-Yanks kind of hatred. And unfair. I've spent a large part of my life fighting militarism. During Vietnam, I was terrified that the war would go on until Dennis was of draft age. I carried on about it, even orating at a dinner party one night at our home that I would "shoot off one of his toes so he won't have to go." Dennis overhead this and told me the next morning that I had made him nervous.

He thought I might suddenly appear, gun in hand, and demand he remove his shoes to give me a clear shot at his toes. "That was just talk," I told him. "I couldn't hurt you." But short of hurting him, I would do anything to keep him safe. I believe having Dennis is the only thing I've done with my life that I have never had one single regret about.

PHEBE

I arose early to go into the garden. My wild excitement of yesterday has turned into listlessness. My moods on this trip are not much different from those at home, just heightened. I used to attribute my sadness to the state of my marriage. Now I think the sadness comes from the fact that I did leave and am consequently husbandless.

A sister in a long white dress came out to cut roses. She smiled, said, "Good morning," as she bent over my table to show the roses to me. I leaned over to smell them and exclaimed over their beauty. She reminded me of Sister Lily, a deaconess friend of my parents. Whenever she came to visit, she brought a bouquet of lilies.

During dateless periods at Augsburg (all the returning WWII vets seemed either to be married or eager to date Deaconess Hospital nurses), I was attracted by Sister Lily's life of selfless service. I had looked forward to Augsburg because my father had assured me I'd meet many "nice Christian boys." But it didn't happen. So when a missionary from Madagascar spoke during Religious Emphasis Week, I decided God was calling me to be a nurse-deaconess. Luckily, I got such bad grades in chemistry it was clear I wouldn't make it through nurses training. I switched to English as my major and settled for being a teacher.

Is it too late for me to become a deaconess? I don't think they're forbidden to marry, but I'm sure they're expected to refrain from sexual activity while in the order. Well, there's a subject I've been avoiding—sex. All my life I've been afraid of sex and eager to engage in it at the same time. I refused to hitchhike through Europe with my Norwegian boyfriend, summer of 1950. I'd come to feel safe in Olso with my daily routine: taking the trolley to buy flowers, bread, and cheese every morning at the farmers market, writing letters home in my room at the Study Center for Young Girls, visiting private social welfare agencies, my study project for the summer. Evenings my boyfriend and I walked across the street to the park to hear accordion bands play. The routine kept me safe from his demands that we "go all the way." If we traveled together, I knew I couldn't resist for long.

MAY 31

JOAN

Our day for the Vatican Museums and Sistine Chapel. It was so incredible I'm still reeling. The richness, the richness. It's really many museums here, more than a week's worth to see everything. We decide just to go to the Renaissance rooms and can't even do them justice in a day. One beautiful chapel is by Fra Angelico, done for Pope Nicholas V. The four Raphael Rooms were done for Pope Julius II and I think they must surely be the most beautiful rooms in the world. Until we enter Michelangelo's Sistine Chapel. The story is that after Raphael saw the first section of the Sistine ceiling unveiled, he admired Michelangelo so much, he adopted his painting style. He also included a portrait of Michelangelo in one of his rooms. It seems fortunate beyond believing that the Vatican had two artists of this caliber working here at the same time.

Another story we heard was that Michelangelo, already well into his 60's, didn't really want the commission of the chapel ceiling and the painting, "Last Judgment," on the wall behind the altar. A rival of his, a minor painter now forgotten, pushed so that Michelangelo would be forced to take both jobs. The painting was completed in 405 days; it's immense, perfect. And then you look up and see the ceiling, the face of God, stretching out that one finger towards Adam.

The restoration work was going on while we were there, and I can understand why it was so controversial.. The old parts are hard to see, obscured by age and the smoke from centuries of candles. But the new, freshly cleaned parts, seem artificial in their bright colors, almost gaudy. Is this how they looked originally? I suppose we'll never know.

After the Vatican Museum, we went racing through the Papal Library pausing here and there to marvel at what one of my non-Catholic friends calls the obscene wealth of the Catholic Church. For instance, a kneeler given by the Dames of Genoa to Pope Leo XIII appears to be rosewood covered tightly with gold and precious stones. Some of the gifts are funny. One is a rock from the moon given to Pope John 23rd by the United States but signed by R. Nixon in such way that it looks as though he personally collected it from the moon and gave it to the Pope.

The Papal Gardens are full of fountains and what looks like Roman ruins and they go on and on and on. Like so many things in Rome, they are magnificently excessive.

Talked to Bob last night after the most frustrating time of my life at the pay phone. Finally a nun took pity on me and put the call through. I shouldn't have bothered because all we did was discuss the missing letter situation. Tonight I was up in the garden writing in my journal and the maid came out with a fat envelope. Inside were copies of Bob's letters #3 and #4 and a new #5. Where the originals of #3 and #4 are is a mystery and #2 seems to have disappeared forever, sunk like my hopes of ever getting Bob to do something the easy, simple, workable way. My way.

PHEBE

We're lingering over lunch, writing postcards and gathering strength for the Vatican Museum and for St. Peter's. Rome is my favorite city thus far—exuberant, richly-layered, ancient and wise. I feel totally at home here. I want to be Italian.

Joan just pointed out to me that two monsignors were walking by. Then she added, "Or they may be cardinals. Though I doubt they'd just be WALKING down the street like that if they were cardinals." She paused for a few seconds and went on, "Well, I didn't mean to imply they'd be FLYING, but..."

We went to mass at St. Peter's. Right during the service, Joan turned to me and spoke sharply, said I'd ruined her shopping bag. Our bags are important. We use them on our daily treks to hold essentials like water, fruit and bread for our thrifty picnics. She thought I'd scrunched too closely to her precious bag and was outraged. "You've punctured it," she said, "and now it's useless." "I've noticed something about Catholics through the years," I whispered to her. "What is that?" she asked, irritated. I answered, "That Catholics think nothing of whispering right during mass. I've noticed it before in your churches. Look at all the people around us, talking and even laughing. But I suppose you're so used to the ritual, you don't think you have to pay attention to it. My father used to preach against the cold formalism of the Catholic Church and now I know what he meant." Right after I said it, I knew I'd gone too far. I apologized. She said, "Oh, I didn't think you meant it. I don't take you seriously when you spew out your anti-Catholic remarks!"

JUNE 1
JOAN

This morning Phebe did a huge wash. It's so nice to be able to hang it out in the walled yard here and not have to drape it around and in front of our windows as we've done in the other towns. Then we went to mail our box of collected guide books, prints, postcards, notebooks and literature home. It's almost to the point where we can't get our suitcases shut for all the paper goods we both love to collect.

Mailing the box became for me a microcosm of how Italy works. Well, operates then. If I could understand what we went through to mail a package home, I could probably live here happily. We felt we became almost Italian in the process. It's the same process that makes cashing a check a two-hour job in Italy, a job that allows me to meet a half-dozen Italian bankers and clerks each time.

It started with finding a box, finally provided by Sister Gabrielle and wrapped so carefully and with such stout twine, I felt sure it could make it to the moon without damage. Next we had to find a Tabac where a storekeeper would put sealing wax on our package. Without this wax, postal people will not give packages insurance, we were told. I asked someone, why a Tabac? "Why not," was the answer, with a shrug for my slowness.

We took a bus to the main post office hoping to find a Tabac on the way. We tried to ask some women on the bus if they knew of one and got a torrent of Italian in return, only two words of which I understood, "Capisce niente? Capisce niente." She understands nothing.

We finally found a Tabac who received our package as though it contained animal filth and in another spate of Italian seemed to say that we had wrapped the package all wrong, he would have to rewrap it before he could put any wax on, we were incredibly lucky he was willing to soil his hands on such a disastrous and stupid project and it was going to cost dearly. It did. Next stop the post office where the package was weighed by one man, money figured and stamps applied by a second and finally $36 for postage taken from us by a third. All in all, it took nearly the entire morning to mail the package home. And everyone we have talked to in Rome says we will be lucky to ever see it again.

We were so exhausted at this point, that we turned around and went back to Villa Rosa for a lie-down. There was nothing much else to do then anyway as Rome closes up tight as a tick between 1 and 3 pm, not counting the restaurants. We can't shop, we can't sightsee. So we might as well take a nice rest so that we can stay up for a late supper like Romans do. We're careful to get home before they leave work and school at 1 pm. The buses are sardine-packed then as all of Rome heads home.

We were already somewhat used to the Byzantine way of doing business in Italy, having had to cash some traveler's checks in Monterossa. In Rome it's even worse. There are two doors to pass through to get into a bank. You open the first door and you are then in an air lock so that guards can look you over before they open the second door. Only one person at a time is allowed through. Once inside, you visit four tellers to cash one check—one takes the check, one studies your passport, a third writes out an order to pay and the fourth teller actually gives you your money.

"If it had been this hard to cash a check in Minnesota," Phebe said, "I'd probably still have that first checking account."

"As I recall, and recall with horror," I said, "that was the account where your fines for Checks Returned for Insufficient Funds were bigger than your paycheck. And where you ran up a Ready Reserve that's still talked about at banking seminars."

After that fiasco, Phebe had a meeting with her family where she admitted to being out of control financially and in front of them cut up each and every one of her credit cards. Unfortunately, she found the next week that our little local drug store would allow her to charge and by the end of the month had a bill for over $300 in Sundries. How can I let her go to Oslo without me?

PHEBE

Here I am in the convent garden again, sweet morning peace. I have picked up a Bible from one of the reading tables and begun reading the Psalms. I found the one the Pope read from the other day, verse 9 of Psalm 139: "If I were to take the wings of the dawn and dwell in the remotest part of the sea, even there Thy hand would lead me and Thy right hand would take hold of me."

This verse certainly is a reminder that no matter how far from home I go, I am always guided by some mysterious being. Why else has this trip been such a time for reflection on my life and where I should go with it next? Maybe I should show a little trust that I can make it on my own. Maybe as soon as I get home, I should find a lawyer and file for divorce.

When I came down in the garden a little after six, the door was heavily barred. I didn't dare open it for fear I'd do it wrong and perhaps awaken the gardener or Sister Gabriel, who would come and scold me for being up so scandalously early. How ridiculous for a fifty-six-year-old woman to be so fearful. Fifty-six years old. Am I really? Where did it all go? Our lives like grass and flowers. Ephemeral. So much of it I simply wanted to "get through." I kept waiting for the "real life" to begin. That was the real life. But what was it? I remember when I read *Zen Mind, Beginners Mind*. That's when I first ran across the lines: "Before enlightenment, chop wood and carry water. After enlightenment, chop wood and carry water."

In the end, I'm brought back to the here and now and the need to pay total attention to it, to the gardener patiently sweeping dead leaves and rose petals and bird droppings off the patio tiles. But I'm also brought back to other nows, to the now of our back yard where I hung all the kids' diapers in the days before dryers or diaper service or disposable diapers. John came out with his camera, took a picture after I'd filled the lines. Not a picture of me working, but the finished product, the diapers themselves. Guess he liked the pattern they made on the lines.

I spent more than 30 years trying to figure him out. Waste of time. One simply breathes in and out. Chops wood and carries water. Sweeps a dirty kitchen floor. Scours out baby shit from birdseye cotton diapers—the excrement gets hopelessly caught in the fine weave of threads. One bends intently over the toilet bowl—these diapers must be spotless—no stain can be allowed to linger.

Here I am in a convent garden in Rome writing about baby shit.

JUNE 2
JOAN

The Pantheon, 143 feet high, 143 feet across, must be the most nearly perfect building in the world to architects and artists of all cultures and surely the most beautiful space I've ever been. I felt sanctified just walking in. I sank down in awe, couldn't speak, just prayed. The Pantheon was a temple of Agrippa, now turned into a Roman Catholic Church which, the guidebooks say, is what saved it from destruction. This is hard to believe because among other desecrations, Pope Urban ordered the removal of 43,000 pounds of bronze from the ceiling, which he gave to Bernini who used it in his famous altarpiece in St. Peter's.

There's a hole in the ceiling, 30 feet across, and light and air pour through it in a great, golden band. Otherwise it's very dark and cool here, the ancient, holy coolness of the centuries. There are many altars and burial crypts around the sides. Statues of important Roman deities were worshipped in these side altars, as was an enormous statue of Jove in the center. Now the altars are filled with Christian saints. The crypts hold famous Romans like young Raphael and his fiancee, who died three months before he did, and Victor Emmanuel II, whoever he is. Why don't I have a better grasp of history at my age? Why do I know as I sit here that I will never look up Victor Emmanuel II in the encyclopedia when I get home no matter how much I promise myself I will at this moment?

After an expensive lunch, we walk and walk, lost most of the time. At one point, Phebe is overjoyed because she has found a familiar street so we cannot be lost after all. The sign says Senso Unico, which means One Way in Italian. I laugh so hard she gets very huffy indeed. It reminds me of a trip to Florida when my friend was overjoyed to find the same street that ran right by his house in Minnesota, probably the longest street in the world he figured, good old Frontage Road.

It is really hot today, over 90, we heard. The sweat rolls off us as we trudge up and down the hills of Rome but we notice that a miracle has occurred. All the walking we've done today, perhaps 15 miles, and our backs haven't hurt once. We have walked our way back into health. It's funny how much farther you can walk when you're a tourist heading for the next sight than you ever could at home.

We did a lot of touristy things today. Threw coins in Trevi Fountain. Shopped around the Spanish Steps for leather coin purses for gifts. Then we had a hamburger and fries at McDonalds, which is located next to the Steps. There was a soldier with a machine gun and no sense of humor out in front. We have noticed soldiers stationed in front of all American stores, banks, and airlines here. The Italian government fears reprisals for our bombing of Libya. I certainly don't blame them for their fear since Italy is a scant 150 miles from Libya.

The terrible atomic accident at Chernobyl also happened right before we left for Europe and radioactive clouds drifted over all the countries we're visiting which means little fresh produce, among other things. The farmers here had to plow under their crops so no artichokes, asparagus, tomatoes, tender green beans.

"I wish the Italians were also protesting the Russians," I said to Phebe, "I hate not having those vegetables, tastes that mean Italy to me."

"Joan, how shallow," Phebe said at her most priggish, "to be thinking of your stomach instead of the poor people in the path of the fallout from that accident."

Two ancient priests from Dublin sitting with us in the Villa Rosa garden shot me a withering look, smiled benevolently at Phebe and said, "Sure and what a sweet girl you are."

We had dinner at the convent tonight, delicious, simple, homemade. Mushroom soup, fresh fish, tiny, new potatoes, herbed carrots, oranges for dessert, and a huge bottle of wine for each table. Lovely. We all went up and sat in the garden, the nice couple from Dungarven, their son, a priest, who's heaven, the two ancient priests and that Sweet Girl I'm traveling with. A nice chat and off to bed. God bless this peaceful place, Rome would be so hard without it.

JUNE 3
PHEBE

I'm reading *The Caravaggio Connection* by Oliver Banks. He says Rome is like a drug, that people come here as tourists and then become addicted to the city, stay on indefinitely, take any part-time job they can find, anything to avoid leaving. Banks writes: "Years later they would still be here, impoverished, apparently happy, leading aimless lives with no goal other than to maintain a marginal existence in the city. Dolce fa niente."

Sweet doing nothing. I'm too old for that sort of romantic nonsense, but Rome does have an incredible hold over me already. I do feel strangely at home here. Part of that feeling, of course, comes from the comfort of staying at the Villa Rosa.

Here we are in the Roman Forum, seated in the shade on ancient Roman rocks, eating our picnic lunches. We're in front of the Temple of Antoninus and Faustina, built by Antoninus in honor of his wife. Here they lie, together forever.

Another worry—where am I going to be buried? Now that I'm a grass widow—yes, that's what my father called divorcees—I can no longer count on being buried alongside my husband. Do I really care? My father and real mother are buried side by side in Sacred Heart cemetery, even though they were only married ten years. I often wondered how my stepmother felt about that since she was married to him for forty years. A bit unfair to my stepmother? After all these years, am I softening towards her? She tried to do what was right. I think she meant well even when she sent me a set of snapshots in full color taken of my father in his casket. They dropped out of a birthday card I received from her a few months after he died.

JOAN

A wonderful breakfast and chat with our Irish friends. There's great excitement. One of the nun's twin sisters is coming with her family for a visit. After breakfast, we go back to our room to write in our journals and get ready for the day. There's a carnival going on in the schoolyard next door and we open our shutters and hang out the windows to marvel at the exuberance below. It's just like school carnivals at home except ten times the talk, the laughter, the life, the excitement. It's games, pony rides, bocce, food, fun Italian style. Con brio.

Today we did Ancient Rome in 95° degree heat. We started with a walk up to the Capitol on Capitolino Hill. One-hundred-seventy-two steps to S. Maria D'Aracoeli. There was a choir singing Gregorian chant as we stumbled in from the sun. The church was cool, filled with crystal chandeliers, built on the highest point of the Capitol, the rock of the citadel of Rome, and probably 11th Century.

Next the Piazza del Campidoglio designed by—who else for such symmetry and beauty but—Michelangelo. The statues in front are enormous, the square composed of two great art museums and the mayoral palace, a great example of Michelangelo as architect, with a bell tower behind and a gorgeous fountain in the middle. This is where non-traditional Romans marry and there were two wedding parties there while we toured, a beautiful bonus for our sightseeing.

Behind this square is an incredible view down and over the Forum. There is a lot of restoration going on but enough remains

uncovered, and the scope of it took my breath away. Now I want to read everything I can get my hands on about Rome. Phebe read something last night about the seductive powers of Rome. People come here to do one tiny piece of research and end up staying for years. They're everywhere, taking tours in English, doing whatever they have to do so that they can stay in Rome. I can see why.

You turn a corner and you're in a different world, 500 years earlier than the street you left. History here is something you can feel, an incredible building of one civilization right on top of another and another. There are modern buildings next to Renaissance palaces next to Roman arches. Nothing is lost, nothing is torn down. You feel as though you might just meet an Etruscan or two if you looked for them hard enough. The way Detective Roderick Alleyn saw them looking out from contemporary Roman faces in the mystery I'm reading here, *When In Rome* by Ngaio Marsh.

The Capitolino museums are handsome and full of statues I've seen copies of all my life, such as the great Etruscan she-wolf (500 BC), plus the Capitolino Venus, Young Boy With Thorn, Dying Gladiator,

Love and Psyche. As we walked down the grand staircase to the Piazza Venezia, the busy center of modern Rome, we passed a cage that is supposed to hold Rome's mascot, a she-wolf. It was empty.

We walked down the hill and around to the entrance of the Forum where we spent hours wandering through the ruins in the hot sun. The Temple of Julia and Temple of Augustus. The prettiest was the Temple of the Vestal Virgins with reflecting pools, roses, roses everywhere and dozens of mainly headless statues. The most touching was the Temple of Antoninus and Faustina. When she died young, Antoninus built this temple for her telling his Roman subjects "I would rather live in the desert with her than in my palace without her." He declared Faustina a Goddess, forcing Romans to worship her. Now there's a husband! We had a picnic lunch looking over this temple and I brooded that perhaps the only way to keep a husband's romantic love alive forever is to die young. Faustina would never have the sagging breasts, stretch marks and lumpy arms of a fifty-year old woman. Where, oh, where are the temples for us?

Another hot walk to the Colosseum. Sitting here, it's easy to imagine 50,000 Romans screaming for blood. The cages for the wild animals are still here and the underground passages used by the humans facing those animals. Every Sunday, Catholic Mass is offered for the souls of the early Christian martyrs, here where they died. It happened nearly 2000 years ago, but in Rome it's as though it happened yesterday.

It's eerie, haunting even, in the hot afternoon sun. Or maybe the idea of cruelty is particularly hard to accept because of the bright sun, the blue sky, the peaceful breezes. On such a day a madman could come into your fast food place with a submachine gun, or a good mother might decide to put her baby down for a final, never-ending nap. And the sun goes on shining.

PHEBE

Sitting here in the sun after wandering around the crumbling ruins of past splendor, I feel that "sweet doing nothing" come over me. To linger here, especially since we've found shade, seems more important than going on to see more tourist sights.

I pick a small flower to press into my journal and imagine it grew from a seed whose ancestor was around back in ancient Roman times, those times I felt so vividly present when I looked at the pictures and read the Latin in my 10th grade textbook.

So much history here, more than a lifetime could discover. The other day we were on our way to the post-office. I was carrying a thirty-pound box of books on my head, the only way to carry it without further damaging my back. We came upon manhole covers marked SPQR and Joan insisted we stop and examine them. I wanted to say, "Why? Are they important?" but my box of books was so heavy, I was only too happy to rest for a moment. Besides, I remembered Oliver Banks had written about these manhole covers, how they're inscribed with the same insignia, Latin for "The Senate and the People of Rome," that was stamped on the lead pipes of the ancient Roman aqueducts. Those water systems still supply the city.

Here, too, is where Gibon first got the inspiration to write his masterpiece.

"It was at Rome, on the fifteenth of October 1764, as I sat musing amidst the ruins of the Capitol, while the barefooted friars were singing vespers in the temple of Jupiter, that the idea of writing the decline and fall of the City first started to my mind."

JOAN

After dinner, Sister Gabrielle let us shop her little store. She is so trusting. After opening everything up, including the cash box, she leaves us alone to shop. So we stocked up on decals, medals, crosses, holy pictures and then put quite a bit of lire in the poor box. There's something about living with such absolute goodness that makes me feel better about myself, about the whole human race.

They're hard on themselves, easy on everyone around them, these nuns. Sister Marietta was telling us how early she had to get up, caught herself, and started to laugh. "Now that you know what a martyr I am," she said, "please tell everyone—she's a right martyr." Sister Gabrielle got bitten by the guard dog yesterday, one she raised from a six-inch pup. She's in pain but continues to work and won't consider punishing the dog. "He's a mean brute; it's just his nature," she says. "But isn't he handsome and a grand guard dog, grand."

I can't get over the luck we had in finding this convent. Rome isn't a city where I would want to rent a room in a hotel. It is so complicated, so large, so historic, so layered, so shouting, so nervous that

I feel the need to find a corner to crawl in where I can feel safe and get a little sleep.

I certainly hope I'll be back here, with these darling nuns and with my dear friend Phebe, in spite of the fact that I have been quite horribly jealous of her ever since we got here. She has ingratiated herself with everyone and they fawn over her. Indeed I think they're convinced that she's just about to convert. For her part, Phebe is acting very pious, which she tells me is a natural part for a parson's daughter.

There were always girls like her at Holy Angels. We more worldly girls called them the Nuns-In-Training, among other less printable names. They would stay on their knees for hours after receiving Communion, rapt in the Lord. They never talked on the bus during our annual week-long retreat. They didn't smoke or meet boys out behind the garages, and they told the nuns on those of us who did "for our own good."

PHEBE

We've just had another delectable meal here at the Villa Rosa, prepared by the sisters—baked chicken, oven-browned potatoes, zucchini-tomato saute, strawberries and cream. Ah, home food, comfort food. We sat at the table again with our Irish friends and their son the priest, who looks like some movie star from the nineteen forties, maybe Cary Grant.

I adore this priest. When I told Joan I was in love with him, never mind the age difference, she said the age difference wasn't the problem. "He's a priest, you know. Come to your senses, woman!" I had to admit I do have this proclivity for getting crushes on ministers. Something sexy about the spiritual man, I've always felt. She was hideously embarrassed to hear me even discussing it in jest. Therein lies the real difference between Catholic and Lutheran. At Bible Camp we teen-age "Christian" girls used to lie in our bunk beds, endlessly discussing the camp pastors we had crushes on. They were the objects of our innocent sexual fantasies and we thought nothing of it.

After dinner, Joan and I went to the little room where all the religious gifts and souvenirs are kept. I went wild, bought crosses, rosaries, Papal seals, pens, keyrings, small statues of the Virgin, stickers with holy emblems. Joan thought I was going too far when I started talking about color-coordinating the tiny fake jewels in the crosses with my blouses and skirts.

My penchant for things Catholic has peaked here in Rome. I even began a small (well, actually, quite grandiose) fantasy about how I would go to the seminary when I got back to the States, become a Lutheran minister, then a "bigwig" in the synod. Eventually, I would bring Lutherans back to the Mother Church. By the time I was seventy, I would be elected first American woman Pope. Then I'd get to wear real jewels, not fake ones like those in the little crosses I bought a few minutes ago in the gift shop. Joan wouldn't be able to call me sacrilegious when I color coordinated my real jewels with my clerical robes.

I'm sitting here in the garden letting the evening breezes of Rome ruffle my hair. Wonder if I'd have to cut it if I became Pope, the way nuns have to shave their heads.

At least, that's what we Lutherans always believed. I'd hate to cut my hair. It's the one part of me I've always loved best, so thick and right now so curly. I don't suppose I'd get to have permanents as Pope, either. But why not? I could do whatever I wanted.

I can see the headlines: "Pope Gets Perm."

JUNE 4

JOAN

I am feeling so at home now in Europe. I'm sure I could live here, especially the hill towns/beaches/cities of la bella Italia, everyone's second country. We got a late start this morning because we waited for Father Edmond's Mass. He's been here a year, studying at the Vatican. Probably because the nuns here are Dominicans from Ireland, all of their paying guests this summer are Irish. Yes, even Phebe.

Lucky for me I love the Irish so much as I am now living with one. Phebe has gone completely Gaelic and speaks most of the time in a thick brogue that only the nuns seem to be able to understand. God knows I can't. She has also taken to wearing Miraculous Medals and Crosses and has bought dozens of them to color-coordinate with her every outfit. I'm pretty sure the nuns don't realize this or they wouldn't keep selling them to her. She is also talking of "turning" Catholic.

I decided to become a nun once, right after seeing *The Bells of St. Mary's*. Actually, I think what I really wanted was to be Ingrid Bergman playing a nun. I was about ten years old and sincere enough about my calling to actually rise from my bed five weekdays in a row to go to early, early Mass.

Finally my Mother asked me what was going on. I'm sure she thought I must have some horrendous sin on my soul to be plying God with so much girlish attention.

"I have decided," I simpered, "that I have been called. Called to become a nun." A sound left my mother's lips, halfway between a snort and a squeal. I realize now she was trying heroically not to laugh. If she had, I might have tried to prove something to her and to myself by continuing with my vocation. Feeling I had been taken somewhat seriously, my calling didn't make it past the next Monday morning and early, early Mass.

PHEBE

Joan and I have gone to sit in the garden before breakfast. After last night's rain everything is fresh, the sky intensely, purely blue. Ah, the much-written-of Rome light. Doesn't seem hot yet, but it never does in this garden. How I love it here. How I'll miss it when we leave. The back wall separates us from the schoolyard. The other night the children and their parents had a little carnival with music, dancing, games, a bonfire. We could see them from our room. How strange to think ordinary life goes on in the cities where one is a tourist. It's these glimpses I think I love the most. They don't make me homesick so much as they make me feel at home.

Later, on our way to the Villa d'Este we saw an advertisement on a billboard for a language school: "It's a sin not to learn languages. We specialize in the teaching of Italian for foreigners." Joan and I resolve to sin no more, to come back and really learn Italian.

The Villa d'Este was a soothing haven from the heat of Rome. I didn't feel like writing anything in my journal nor did I try to draw the incredible fountains. I'm sure I'll regret that later, but I bought lots of postcards. Then I simply gave myself over to the many paths and drenched statues and mist-filled air. It was all a watery dream where my Piscean soul could have settled in forever. I absorbed it all, resolving as I always do, to come back someday soon. Resolving to find out all I can about Lizst who spent time there composing music. Resolving to find out more about my favorite statue, Diana of Ephesus.

JOAN
(VILLA D'ESTE)

Villa d'Este could only be Italian. Grandiose, intimate, and incredibly beautiful. Built by a Cardinal, son of Lucretia Borgia, it is an  amazing engineering feat with water, water everywhere, somehow falling and spraying and re-circulating to fall and spray again without the use of electricity. But I forgot the structure and genius of the design, I was so overcome by its beauty. Walking down the long paths bordered and crowned by water, the light is green and dim, shadowed by the trees and shrubs. Walk into the light and the water sparkles and glimmers and dances, a thousand colors, rainbow-lit by the sun. There was always a suggestion of cool mist on my skin. What an elegant way of slowing down, especially on a hot, hot day like today.

We had a wonderful *al fresco* lunch amid the pools and waterfalls and fountains. It's over 90 today but all this water made it seem cooler. We stopped and bought sandwiches, cream-filled pastries and cookies for a little over $7. Yesterday we bought just the ingredients for lunch—bread, cheese, meat and fruit for less than $3. Sure beats eating out in Rome. Our lunch in the square in front of the Pantheon was $18 and was both scanty and indifferent. That was one of the first lessons for us, travelers without megabucks. Never, never eat at a cafe located in a famous square. Go around the block and eat where the Romans do.

JUNE 5

PHEBE

Back in the Villa Rosa garden again, where I've just had a brief conversation with a little boy who's staying here with his parents. He asked me, "Are you descended from anyone famous?" and I said, "No, are you?" He replied, "Yes, I have an aunt who's a film actress." I didn't get a chance to ask him who she was, because he was suddenly off playing with his ball, throwing it against the wall. It went over into the little enclosure where the vicious dog hangs out, the one that bit Sister Gabriel. She's not afraid of him, though. She came right out and retrieved his ball.

At the mass this morning in the little convent chapel, the young Irish priest officiated and his parents read the lessons. Only a few of us there—Joan and I, the two women who teach in a Christian Brothers school in Ireland and the convent nuns. I was very moved by the mass, despite my slight feeling of unease, of not really belonging. Certainly no one made me feel that way. He offered prayers not only for his parents but specifically for us, the American travelers, and of course he gave thanks for the sisters and their hospitality. Everyone had a chance to add intercessions of their own and I wanted to, but was afraid Joan would think me out of line, presuming to be Catholic too soon. It was all so intimate and beautiful. I felt I'd been there for a lifetime and therefore, it was very sad to say goodbye to them all, knowing I may never see them again.

My father would have added, "But we'll meet again in heaven." Or maybe he wouldn't, in this case, since they're all Catholics, including, at least right now, me.

JOAN

Sitting out among the roses in the garden of the Villa Rosa, I'm letting my hair and clothes dry in the soft, fresh breeze. It's so peaceful, it seems as though I could get my whole life figured out before supper at seven. I am going to hate to say goodbye to these Irish nuns tomorrow, especially Sister Gabrielle. I wonder if I'll ever again sit in this garden I love so much and whether she will be here. She leaves soon for England and what the Dominicans call Renewal, a time of prayer, study, and rest. She doesn't think she needs a rest and I don't think she needs more spirituality. She's a doer, prays while talking and scrubbing, and she couldn't get any closer to God, in my opinion. But I could. Perhaps I should come back here for my Renewal. Surely in this holy place I would know what my life has been worth so far and what I can do with the rest of what's left to me. But right now the bell is ringing for supper.

EVENING : We sat in the garden after supper, letting the very last light of our very last evening here pale and turn dark. And still we sat, inhaling the roses, sitting in a soft spill of light from the nuns' sitting room above, listening to their soft Irish voices floating down to us in what must surely be a Roman dream.

9. FRENZY IN FIRENZE
Sorry, Florence is closed

JUNE 5
PHEBE
(TRAIN TO FLORENCE)

W e're experiencing a slight slow-down. I should be used
to the slowness of Italian trains, but I get nervous
when we slow down too much. Reminds me of riding a train
through Canada with Rolf after his sophomore year at Reed.
We'd only gotten as far as Kamloops, British Columbia, when
the train stopped. We were left languishing in the car almost
all day with no information. Finally, we found out a wildcat
strike was holding us up. We were transferred to buses that
took us the rest of the way to Winnipeg.

I love how trains allow you time to let your mind wander.
Or time to simply stare out the window. I've always done both
very well. I remember when the children were all finally in
school, how I'd sit alone with my mug of morning coffee, on
a high red metal stool by the radiator in the kitchen, soaking

up the warmth, daydreaming, looking out the window at the snow-lavished lilac bushes. Sometimes a small brave chickadee would land so close I could almost see his eyes. I'd muse about what my life had come to—housework, husband, children. Was that all there was to be? Why wasn't my husband finishing graduate school so I could realize my ambition of being a college professor's wife? Why did I sometimes feel so useless and out of the mainstream, despite all the volunteer work I did and all the dinners I carefully planned and served to our friends? Was more mothering the answer?

For a while I thought it was. One day while Erik was watching TV, he saw a public service announcement urging people to take in foster kids. "Mom, can we take in some kids?" I called the agency. Before I knew what had happened, we had two little boys living with us. Now I had no time to worry that life was passing me by.

JOAN

En route to Firenze: We're on a very fast, very cold, very early train after a bad night where we both woke up a lot. We felt safe at the Villa Rosa and we got tense when we had to move on. Sign of our age, I suppose. Nesting in, turning little routines into comfortable ruts. It's good for people our age to throw themselves boldly into the unknown often.

Sister Gabrielle said she'd get up and make coffee for us at 6:30 and there she was in her pink chenille robe looking like an angel. It was harder than I had imagined saying goodbye to Villa Rosa, to all the dear nuns and especially to Sister Gabrielle. She said she'd offer her Mass for us this morning. She told someone at dinner last night, "Those two, they've made friends with everyone here." This morning she unlocked and opened the heavy outer door, hugged and kissed us both, and said "Goodbye darlings and God Bless." We both mumbled something through our tight throats. We were leaving home, after all.

And now we're off to the unknown again this morning, heading for that golden city dreaming in the sun along the Arno. I must have read that somewhere, but where? Anyway, on to Florence, city of Renaissance princes and popes. I wish I had read a good history of the Medicis before I left home.

Ah, the old desire to be an intellectual sweeps over me again. Luckily my natural sloth nowadays keeps me from doing anything about it. Years ago as young marrieds, Phebe and I both aspired to the Bright Life. We used to have endless discussions about literature, especially William Faulkner who was then my personal favorite. Phebe said she didn't like his writing and was always putting him down. We argued for years until one night at a cocktail party the truth came out. The only thing that Phebe had ever read of Faulkner's was one short story, "A Rose For Miss Emily." And instead of cravenly apologizing, she announced haughtily that she felt she had gotten the true flavor, the gist of the man's work from this one short story. She insists to this day that he is highly overrated. And she still has not read one more word by Faulkner. It drives me batty.

The Italian hill country we're riding through should be sketched, not written about. I want to be able to do it and find I can't. Should I take some drawing lessons too? Phebe says I'd get better if I took lessons. But I doubt it. You can't even tell my cows from my mountains in the sketches I've tried.

I remember the most horrible day in grade school was always the one where Sister turned to the class and said, "I have a treat for you, children. This afternoon we're going to spend doing ART. You may all draw a beautiful Christmas scene for your parent's Spiritual Bouquet." The nuns talked about ART in capital letters and about MUSIC the same way. We were to respect these things. And be a little afraid of them too. God knows I was.

As soon as the word ART left Sister's mouth, panic seized me. Humiliation lay just hours ahead. Oh, I tried, how I tried. Grasping one of my new crayons from a set of Birney & Smith 48s, I would bear down hard. I always drew the manger scene, Mary, Joseph, and Jesus. It always looked like a tiny snake in a blanket between two vultures.

PHEBE

Not only am I unable to stop buying books, I've taken to picking up stones, very small ones, but nevertheless stones, from each of the places we visit. Joan thinks it quite silly, but I try to persuade her it's a good idea by emphasizing how cheap they are. Well, free actually. Of course, I already have forgotten which stone represents which place. The whole project is laughable, unless I figure out some simple way of identifying them, short of writing on the stones themselves. I could number them and then write more elaborate descriptions in my journal.

Here I am at the Cathedral of Santa Maria di Fiore. I want to write "Holy Mary, Mother of God!" because I can't believe what I see in my guidebook. Joan is not going to believe this synchronicity. Seems that in the year 1099, Pazzino dei Pazzi returned from the Crusades, bringing with him three stones from the Holy Sepulchre. The guidebook goes on to say there was a procession which set out to meet him and place those stones in the church. On Holy Saturday the stones were used to produce the spark from which all the Easter candles in Florence churches were lit. How can she complain about my picking up stones and lugging them all over the continent when a devout Italian Catholic who went on the Crusades did it? Of course, as she pointed out when I asked her that very question, "Those were sacred relics from the Holy Sepulchre. Yours are just stones you've picked up off the street."

The guidebook also says that the government commissioned Arnolfo di Cambio to build a church similar to "a heart swelling to immense grandeur." Oh, how compulsively I copy down all these probably insignificant facts, doubtless missing, as Joan would say if she could see what I'm writing, all the important ones.

We only saw the exterior of the Pitti Palace because it was closed. We wandered in the Boboli Gardens, behind the palace, which was built for the Medici Duke Cosimo and his wife Eleanora of Toledo. I had a strong urge to write "Ohio" after "Toledo." I can't allow myself to give in to such impulses or I might start writing a never-ending story about a cross-cultural and across-the-centuries marriage. Could a five-and-dime store clerk from Ohio find happiness with a wealthy and titled Italian duke?

Anyhow, the Boboli Gardens revived us and we ended up being grateful for the chance to stay outside in the soft Italian air, instead of having to roam through the cavernous rooms with their ancient lingering odors of calumny and treachery. I'm making that up, based on the little I know about the Medicis.

JOAN

The train has come to a complete stop in what seems to be the middle of nowhere. Italian trains are not the ploddingly perfect trains of the other countries we've been in. They have capricious personalities, stopping and starting on apparent whims. We had a fright in Genoa the other day. The railroad workers had voted to strike, which they do on a semi-regular basis. Later the same day they voted not to strike.

In the Rome station I finally stopped and bought a cart with wheels for my suitcase. I can't imagine why I didn't do this days before or indeed why I didn't get one before we left the States. In spite of what I read in travel books, finding a porter in a train station is often impossible. I think travel writers should also mention that if you can't lift your suitcase straight up and over your head when it's all packed, you better take things out. I've had to perform this feat again and again, lifting my luggage to the racks over the seats in trains.

Arrival in Firenze: A funny to-do with the cab driver. He kept arguing, trying to tell me something. With no Italian, all I could do was keep pushing the name and address of our hotel under his nose. Phebe, deep in a map, kept insisting we walk. She was right. Finally, in disgust, the driver threw our bags in the taxi and took us less than two blocks. The hotel was just across and down the street from the station. He was mad because he lost his place in line. I was mad because I paid for a non-ride. Phebe was mad because I didn't listen to her. Oh, for a little language.

In America, a hotel near a train station is likely to be in a horrible part of town. Not so in Europe. This hotel is right across from the station and very comfortable and fairly elegant. When we got to the hotel, Phebe cheaped out. When offered a room with private bath for just $10 more ($5 each) she chose the one with the bath down the hall. Once she gets interested in something, there's no stopping her. Right now it's making her money last through Europe and she's a tiger. I never thought I'd live to see Phebe crouched over cash night after night, figuring and fingering each coin.

Our room is Italian terrific. Big windows with heavy, wooden shutters. High ceilings and marble floors so it seems cool here on this very hot day. Twin beds and a sink in the corner. The bath is  the funniest one I've ever seen. It's tiny, tiny with the shower coming right down on top of the toilet and bidet. I can't say I wouldn't love to stay in a four or five star hotel but this would limit my traveling to about a week a year. Travel magazines would have us believe that only rich Americans can afford Florence. This is a lie. After all, Italians aren't all rich, and when they travel, they need nice hotels. I'll bet there are hotels like this one, clean, pretty, and unpretentious, in every city of Europe.

The first thing I did upon unpacking was a rather large wash which I strung on our handy little elastic line back and forth in front of the opened windows. Phebe said that she feels as though she has seen half of Europe through my underpants. If I didn't wash this often, her other choice would be a traveling companion who smells like a stoat. And it would be her fault. Phebe is always coming up with new medical information, and her latest was that the aluminum in deodorant gets right into your blood stream, races to your brain where it is deposited, causing permanent damage.

I have long been a sucker for any and all of Phebe's pronouncements about health. Years ago she convinced us young mothers that we could increase our children's IQ's by re-training them in crawling. For weeks, we forced our toddlers to crawl a new way, resulting in very unhappy children covered with maroon fuzz from Phebe's carpet. However, all the kids turned out to be really smart so how could I argue with Phebe about health? I threw away all my deodorant before leaving for Europe. The result, in the broiling Italian sun, is not savory. And leads to lots of washing.

Anyway, it's so hot here that the wash should be dry by the time we get back. Then I'll take it down and she can gaze on Florence unimpeded by my panties. Actually, I make myself part of Florence when I hang out my wash. It's the national flag of Italy, this display of clean, drying clothes hanging from every window.

We dumped the rest of our clothes and went off on a real hike. We must have walked 10 miles in the terrible heat because we were walking the wrong direction much of the time. We finally got to the Duomo and it was closed. So was the next door Bapistry.

I hated Florence so much at this point I almost kicked in the doors. Not the famous "Gates of Paradise" Bapistry doors, of course. Half of them were gone, out for "restaurazione" a word I've grown to loathe in Italy. After a long, hot wait, they finally decided to reopen the Duomo. The dome was designed by Brunelleschi and inside are wonderful frescos by Della Robbia. The dome is so perfect Michelangelo said St. Peter's would be bigger but never finer. We lit some candles, said some prayers, and went slowly back to the hotel for a siesta and a read.

After our nap, we headed for the river. On our way to the Arno, it seemed as though we were walking right into the Renaissance, past ancient buildings and squares, beautiful and mysterious.

The Ponte Vecchio (Old Bridge) across the Arno is fascinating. It's a double-decker bridge with houses and shops on both levels. There have been jewelry shops on this bridge for over 600 years. Mom talks in her journal about buying her "good" pearls, (not "real" pearls but "good," another subtle difference between the middle class and the rich) right here on this bridge, sixty years ago.

We walked over the bridge and on to the Boboli Gardens and Pitti Palace and back, another few miles or so but it felt like a hundred. The gardens were lovely but, of course, the museums were closed.

JUNE 6

PHEBE

Today at the Uffizi, I began to observe more closely certain details in each of the paintings, especially hands and the gestures they made. I found myself wanting to draw rather than simply write descriptions.

Once in the early nineteen sixties, I took a drawing course after someone told me the only way to really appreciate art was to learn to draw. I don't know if the course heightened my appreciation of art, but it was quite an experience. We had a seedy young artist for a teacher who drank heavily before he arrived at class and whose disdain for us was quite apparent. We spent hours drawing still lifes, carelessly arranged by him on a high stool a few minutes before we students arrived. Overripe fruit, stained scarves, soiled bottles. He rarely gave us any instruction, but merely passed among us once during the evening to see what we were doing. Then he retreated to the back of the room to smoke.

On the last night of class he had a surprise for us. At least it was a surprise for me. Perched on the stool instead of the still life was a young man wearing a bathrobe. As soon as we'd set up our drawing boards and had our charcoal at the ready, he dropped his robe. I was stunned. It seems odd to me now that I hadn't realized he would be naked under that robe, but I hadn't.

Anyhow, always the good scout (as in Girl Scouts, where I had learned years before never to panic in an emergency), I proceeded to draw more intently and determinedly than I'd ever done before. What I produced was so much better than any of the insipid still lifes I'd turned out on previous evenings. I was especially proud of how well I had captured his penis and balls. They were close to the real things. As was I. As minister's children, we were always instructed to sit in the front pew. Still obedient to that rule, I had seated myself in the front row, close enough to see the veins throbbing. Just writing about it brings a flush to my face.

Time to get serious about the art. Paolo Veronese (1528-1588) painted "Sacra Famiglia con Santa Barbara." Saint Barbara is a saint familiar to me because when the kids were little, we celebrated festivals of the church year in our home. In our book "Festival of Christmas," the author suggested that on December 4, St. Barbara's Day, the mother in the family should cut off a branch from a flowering bush to force blossoms by Christmas. I usually cut off a section of our bridal wreath hedge. We got lots of green leaves, but never any blossoms. A strange ritual to celebrate St.Barbara because years later I found to my horror that she was the matron saint of munitions makers.

Here's Caravaggio's "Sacrificio di Isacco," the story of God's unbelievable command to Abraham to sacrifice his beloved son Isaac. I heard my father preach about Isaac when I was a small child, squirming in the hard wooden pew of the little country church near Monte. My mother had just given birth to my brother David. What if God demanded we kill David the way he demanded Abraham kill Isaac? How could God be so cruel?

Today I bend down to look deep into the eyes of Isaac as he awaits his father's blow. I see no fear, only utter trust. In the eyes of the ram, I see an almost human look as if he were beseeching Abraham, "Here I am. Take me. Spare your son."

JOAN

Machiavellian. That's what the people of Florence are. They have arranged museum and cathedral hours so that you cannot possibly visit even half of what you want to see in one day. This is bitter news for us. We are determined to go not so fast through Europe, but we hate to miss great things because of lousy scheduling. You really can't figure the schedule before you get to a new city in Italy. There doesn't seem to be any rhyme or reason for when they open and close and you can't find out about it until you arrive.

We got up early. Breakfast downstairs was surprisingly good even though there's an old lady whose sole function seems to be to sit in the dining room and keep her evil eye upon us. She isn't serving anything, she doesn't greet anyone, she just sits there and watches every mouthful we take with black, reptilian eyes in a wrinkled, unfriendly face.

She scares me, although I know deep down she isn't a person with enough clout to get me kicked out of the hotel if she doesn't like the way I chew. People who are supposed to help have always intimidated me. Take my cleaning lady. Why do I spend the day before she comes cleaning the house? I wouldn't dream of letting her see it in its usual sty-like condition. I never ask her to do any of the really disgusting things either. As soon as she leaves, I clean the kitty litter box and wash the garbage can myself.

The one I'm really scared of, though, is Gary, our Garbologist. That's how he signs his Christmas cards which he tapes to the top of the garbage can right before Christmas in his not-so-veiled attempt at blackmail. It's been said by the neighbors, and I believe it, that Gary has turned down garbage. Didn't like the looks of it, wouldn't take it.

PHEBE

While eating lunch at the Uffizi, I placed my tired feet on the rung of the chair opposite me. The waiter came over and silently pushed my feet off. I thought he was trying to be funny, but when I looked up at him in amazement, I was greeted by his stern visage. Made me furious since both the two German-speaking women at the next table have their feet on the rungs of the extra chairs. Is this some kind of anti-American discrimination? Is it because the Italians and Germans were allies during World War II? Perhaps I should remind him we Americans landed at Salerno and freed their country from Fascist tyranny.

But how can I be disturbed by such a triviality when I am surrounded by so many great paintings. So many artists I've never heard of, such as Alonso Berruguet (1486-1561) who painted "Madonna con Bambino," a sweet painting of Mary playing with the Baby Jesus. She's tickling his tummy just like mothers have done down through the centuries, and Jesus is laughing. Looking at this painting I got a sudden pang of home- sickness, wishing Caitlin were here. When I get home, I'm going to bring her out to Monte to be with me for a whole week. My own childhood still seems so vivid to me, yet my kids' and grandkids' childhoods seem to go by far too fast, as if in a dream.

JOAN

I was really stiff and sore today and my back hurt so we stopped at a farmacia for aspirin. Phebe found a package of hair color she wanted to try except, when she went to pay for it, it turned out to be a package of condoms.

This made me laugh which was great as I had gotten up feeling crabby and mean. I've been praying lately for a disposition like my dad's, endlessly sweet and patient. Nothing ruffled him. I remember a cold November morning when I came over and found him sitting outdoors in his car, listening to the radio.

I said, "Dad, what are you doing out here? It's really cold."

"Oh, well," he said, "your mom was a little confused this morning. She thought I was just being lazy and insisted that I get going, get dressed, get out and look for a job."

"Didn't you remind her that you were retired and 88 years old?"

"No. When this happens, I just agree, get up and come outside for awhile. Then when I go back in, I say, 'Hi dear, I'm home from work,' and your mom accepts that I've been gone for hours."

"Doesn't this upset you, make you angry?"

"Makes me sad for your mother is all. I'd hate to have her realize how much she's forgotten. She was so smart. And she's so proud."

In the Uffizi Gallery: Room after room of many paintings you've seen copies of, all hung closely together with not a guard in sight and no ropes between you and the paintings. You can get your nose right up to them and no one says a word. A room full of Botticellis. Another crammed with Rembrandts. Then Raphael. A gallery with Phebe's favorite—Caravaggio. I especially liked his wonderful Medusa.

We went up to the restaurant on the roof of the museum for lunch and met a nice couple from Israel. It was a wonderful lunch, speaking English and looking out over the brown and red tiled roofs of Florence. Every tile is different because in the Middle Ages, tiles were formed over a worker's thighs so each is unique— short, long, fat, thin, just like the worker.

When we got down to the street, I realized I had left behind my plastic bag with my journal. The museum was closed and when I begged the guard to let me back in, he shook his head and said, in his only English, no dice, no dice. Finally, I must have looked so desperate that he relented, left his post and we tore together up three flights of stairs to the roof. And there it still was. I showed him my writing and terrible drawings and told him it was all about Italy, tutti d'Italia, and we patted each other and laughed and I wondered how much he understood. No matter. A mille grazie signore.

We spent the afternoon with the Medicis in their little Palazzo Vecchio. Unreal. There's a room that the mad monk Savanarola insisted Cosimo build, big enough to hold the entire Florence city council, 500 strong. It's so huge I think it could hold 5000. In one corner, unpretentiously tucked away and unnoticed except by two students sketching it, "The Victor," by Michaelangelo.

The mad monk Savonarola, a Florentine oddity, was a Dominican, head of the monastery of St. Mark's in the 1500's. He preached against the vanities of the flesh, especially music, art, beauty...everything the people of Florence loved and lived for. One year he burned a huge pile of music, rich clothing and paintings in a bonfire in the Piazza della Signoria in front of the palace. The next year he was burned at the stake in the very same place he had held his bonfire of the vanities.

A long, slow amble home. We stop at the beautiful Bapistry of the Duomo. Amazing! It's open. The Bapistry is a separate, octagonal building in front of the cathedral, most famous for its bronze doors, what Michaelangelo called the "Gates of Paradise" by Ghiberti. Inside, we're awed by the ceiling or dome, all of mosaics. It's very cool in here, a lovely place to stop, think, and write in our journals.

We went shopping at the outdoor market, acres of shopping, hog heaven under tarps, wagon after wagon piled high with goods. You can find almost anything from shoes and jewelry to food and just plain junk. This is where Florence must come to shop, around the ancient Church of San Lorenzo. In the stalls here, the storekeepers are openly insulting, don't seem to care if you buy anything or not. So I don't.

My impressions of Florence so far— hot, dirty, beautiful. Things seem uncared for, they're blase about their treasures. Proud people with no American slang or the touristy stuff we've heard elsewhere. Most places we've been, the people say "no problem, no problem" no matter what you ask. Not in Florence.

Ahh, but the beauty. Art piled in heaps. The colors of Florence, wonderful browns from dun to orangey-red. And the food. Dinner last night at the Trattoria next door started with 8 to 10 different dishes for antipasto, huge bottles of wine and water, then veal in a white wine and lemon sauce. When I got back to the hotel, there were two letters from Bob. Like my whole relationship with him, a surprise, nothing in a pattern.

I talked to Phebe about taking a quick side trip in the Alps after Venice. I really would like to try and find some of my relatives. I preface my request to Phebe by using our pet phrase, "Have I Got A Treat For You!" This is a part of our special language, what I call our Old Friend's Shorthand. It started years ago when one or the other had something to do and didn't want to do it alone. Needed a friend. Like the time Phebe traveled with me to my nephew's graduation in a distant town.

We don't use "Have I Got A Treat For You!" too often but when we do, it's with the certainly that the other will be there and do as asked. We're good friends because we're willing to be there not just for the big days but all the time—all the boring, duty-filled, silly, messy, embarrassing, weird, awful, and just plain ordinary days that make up life.

JUNE 7

PHEBE

At last, what I've been looking forward to—Michelangelo's "David." Leading up to the famous statue itself was an avenue of unfinished statues, which I found exciting because they revealed the process he had to go through in chiseling his masterpiece. I looked at the rough chisel marks with fascination. My guide book says, "Michelangelo wanted to free the soul of suffering humanity which he thought was imprisoned in the stone."

Then, because I wanted to rest awhile, I leaned against a balustrade, very close to the guard who was sitting on a chair. Maybe I could exude such weariness that he would give up his seat so I could sit and write in my journal. Miracle of miracles, he did.

So here at last I'm seated in front of "David." What strikes me is how feminine, how languid, how vulnerable he is. He has massive muscles and enormous hands.

But he has the stance of a young boy, which he was, not that of a warrior, which he wasn't. The sling rests on his left shoulder and he looks casual, unhurried, as if he weren't planning to do anything harmful with that sling.

His heroic proportions seem wrong for the story. Or do they? David was puny and young compared to the giant Goliath, but spiritually he was immense. Michelangelo was perhaps trying to show this quality by making him larger than life.

The David and Goliath story was one of my favorites and one of the few I really understood as a child. Easy to identify with David. In the luridly-illustrated Sunday School folders he was always portrayed as a little boy, much younger than the man Michelangelo sculpted. He was never shown naked, either, but fully-clothed in garish colors we always associated with Palestine, or The Holy Land, as my father called it.

My father identified with David, too, partly because he was named after him. I think he believed he was like the Biblical David, fighting the Goliaths in our Lutheran synod. They didn't have the foresight and vision he did, refusing to give him financial support for his home mission venture in Falcon Heights. "Only cornfields out there. There'll never be enough people to start a church," he was told.

So my father went ahead without synod support. We kids were sent around the neighborhood with mimeographed flyers announcing the first Sunday School and church services to be held in a rented school house. After World War II when many large suburbs grew up, the synod leaders were finally convinced. They were finally ready to admit there was a future in Falcon Heights and began supporting the mission. Now there are three thriving churches, all begun by my father, all testament to his vision.

JOAN

Galleria dell' Accademia. We turn a corner and there, at the end of two rows of unfinished statues by Michelangelo, a glass-domed rotunda and "David." I had heard he was huge but you have no idea of how huge, how impressive until you see him. Mom was right. She said in her journal that his hands are "too big" for his body but they're absolutely wonderful hands, peasant hands. His feet are big, somewhat flat. He's a beautiful boy, one can hardly bear to think of him aging, thickened and corroded into a balding, paunchy man.

I wonder what he's holding in his up-raised hand. Then I remember. A rock, of course. What, if anything, is he thinking with that innocuous, bland look? Pleasant but withdrawn.

A little spoiled? By Michelangelo perhaps. He must have loved David enormously to be able to create this. And what it must feel like to be David, to look at yourself in stone, like this boy did, and realize that you will be beautiful and young and adored for ages. I hope they both knew the marvel of what they had done together, that boy and Michelangelo.

The crowds are so funny. They don't seem to know how to react. Lots of people pose, right in front of David, to have a picture taken. For comparison? So that some of his beauty will rub off on them? What are they thinking?

Museo di San Marco: Surely this is the most peaceful place in Florence, a Dominican Abbey and home to Fra Angelico for many years. He decorated all the monks' cells for them. Some of the paintings are flaked off and nearly gone. Why can't they cover them, save them somehow? How can Florence stand to know that Fra Angelico's "Annunciation" at the top of the stairs is peeling and cracking?

We're sitting down, our favorite tourist pose, in a cool corridor outside the library which has row after row after row of priceless, illuminated manuscripts. It's easy to imagine the seduction of the cloister here, an oasis of peace in Florence, built high and cool around two squares with a statue of St. Dominic and a wonderful old well in the middle.

My sister and I used to fantasize about how much better life would have been if we had joined a nunnery. This was during the days of our individual Marital Troubles. Oh dear, that phrase sounds bad. A little like talking about Female Complaints. Soon Phebe might be deep into Marital Troubles. We've had so many laughs over here that whole days go by and I forget about what I suppose will be the days of sorrow, or at least regret and loss, that are coming to her. I can't believe people who whistle happily throughout a divorce. How can you not regret the loss of someone you once loved enough to marry?

PHEBE

We've arrived at San Marco Museum, the cloister home of Fra Angelico, perhaps my favorite painter of all. The catalog says, "Fra Angelico came out of the religious reform movement in Tuscany...he was said to have been divinely inspired...painting as an angel would without recourse to the adroit deceptions of art."

I love "Last Supper with Cat and Peacock" with all its small everyday objects painted with such loving detail. I'm surprised, though, to see a cat allowed in the house, let alone a peacock. I didn't know people kept pets inside then, but rather left them outdoors to wander freely. Reminds me of a baby pig with whom I shared a rowboat the last time I visited Norway. My cousins from Dale rowed me across the fjord to visit another cousin who lived on the side of a mountain in a grass-roofed hut. We were delivering the pig to the cousin. I stayed overnight in that cozy hut and the pig stayed inside too. He was part of the family, at least until he grew large enough for the slaughter.

I've just told Joan about a mystery I'm reading with a red-haired heroine. "Did you know," I ask her, "that some people believe red-haired people are blessed with extraordinary powers of insight?" Joan wants nothing to do with the supernatural, and I don't blame her. I used to dream I was standing alone by my mother's grave when a long white arm pulled itself slowly through the dirt and reached for me. My mother was trying to claim me for her dark underground kingdom and I didn't want to go. When I woke up, I was sweaty and trembling. Great guilt and sadness overwhelmed me.

10. THE CATS OF VENICE
Rain, romance and the perfect pasta

JUNE 8

JOAN
(TRAIN TO VENICE)

Phebe had bought heavily in the Florence markets and I had not. I spent most of this train ride trying to convince her to sell me some of her booty, especially the beautifully-tooled leather bookmarks she had picked up for a song. I couldn't budge her and the conversation got more and more childish:

Phebe: "No, I won't sell or give you a bookmark."

Joan: "But you have so many. How about just one?"

Phebe: "No. You should have bought your own."

Joan: "Well, Venice will have nicer ones anyway."

Phebe: "Florence is known for leather.   Venice for glass. Perhaps you can find some nice glass bookmarks."

We're sitting in the Bologna station, where it seems we've been for days, on the world's oldest, funniest train. It's pouring rain which should relieve some of the horrible heat that's making us both testy.

We've been watching each other like hawks for signs that one is getting an advantage of any kind over the other.

"Watch it. You're way over the screw with your journal."

The screw is what we have decided is the midpoint of the train's tiny writing desk we're both trying to use. Friendship saved again! We unite in fury at our common enemies, a pair of American ladies who have gotten on the train in Bologna with at least six big pieces of luggage each of which they are trying to push under our seats. Well, we put a stop to that jolly quick. It's funny how quickly Phebe and I can revert to childish behavior. Or maybe it isn't. I still feel the same way as I did when I was 10, and 20, 30, or 40. All those ages are still in there, ready to come out when I need them.

Arriving by train, Venice is a disappointment. There's a very long bridge that seems to go on for miles past ugly, heavy industrial development on the coast. Even inside the station you can see nothing of the romantic canals and bridges. But when you step outside the station, there it all is, spread before you, watery, dreamlike. The Grand Canal is filled with taxi-speedboats, beautiful private boats and great, lumbering vaporettos, the big bus-boats. Steps lead down to the edge of the water where boats wait to take you to your destination. Ours, we're told, is a vaporetto to Via Zaccaria.

Our hotel is right off the Grand Canal, a three-minute walk past the Doges Palace to San Marco Square. The hotel is down a narrow alley, tucked back out of the way, but it's small, charming and best of all, they are holding three letters for me from Bob. The room is lovely and neat but tiny and very dark. The ceiling is made of polished dark logs. It looks out on a small, dank courtyard and the windows are fenced against feral cats. You can see the cats have visited here often as the screen is full of their various furs and the air full of the stench of their spray. Cats, lean and hungry looking, seem to be everywhere in Venice, roaming freely.

They make me lonely for Delilah. Of course she'd hate it here in Venice because she hates cats. Which is unfortunate because she is a cat. Delilah could hold her own here, though, she's the meanest old black cat in the world. She has one ear with hair on it that goes up and one bald ear that goes down. She's covered with scars from many fights, five litters of kittens, and two operations. Delilah can't hear, can't see, and can't remember where her litterbox is kept these days. Which is why the area behind the tree in the dining room smells the way it does. Delilah turned 20 this year, making her the World's Oldest Living Cat, I figure. That's 140 years old, catwise. She looks even worse than these wild Italian cats. She looks like a sorry little victim of Cat Abuse, which she is. I was the abuser, my most awful secret.

I saw her wetting on the couch in my office one day. I flew over and swept her off the couch onto the floor. I must have hooked her in the ear because two days later her ear swelled up and she had to have an operation. And while she was under the anesthetic, she lost control of her bladder and the vet discovered that she had a bad bladder infection. She couldn't tell when or where she was urinating. Oh, Delilah, I'm so sorry. I do love you so. You and I have been together for 20 years; you and I were young together.

Of course, poor Dennis got the worst of it. I was out of town when her ear swelled up and he had to take her to the vet. And when the vet asked what had happened, he lied for me. Told him Delilah had gotten caught by a swinging door.

Dennis has been taking care of me since he could talk. I remember putting him on the bus for kindergarten, feeling pretty blue. "Now Mom," he said, "Don't cry at the bus stop. I'll be home in a little while. You'll be okay." The caretaker. When he was about eight or nine, he was hit by a car driven by his best friend's mother and as they were loading him into the ambulance, all he did was worry about her. "It was my fault, Mom, I rode my bike into the alley without looking. Please don't let the police put her in jail."

I still don't know how he got the two of us safely through his teen years but he did. Teenager. The very word filled me with dread. So many of my friends' kids had discovered drugs, dropped out, run away. I fretted about it constantly until Dennis sat me down one day in the kitchen and told me he wasn't going to get into trouble. And he didn't. It sounds as though I had a Master Plan for the Perfect Kid.

Actually, my mothering skills consisted mainly in thinking Dennis was wonderful. Which I do and which I say often. Among other things, Dennis doesn't criticize me and God knows he could. I'm guilty. I worked outside the home; I didn't always have the time to do things perfectly for him. And he had to do lots of things for himself. But he told me once he'd had a wonderful childhood. I need to believe him, so I do.

PHEBE

I'm in the hotel bathroom, sick to my stomach, unable to sleep. I'm not sick from over-eating, but from the odor of male cat spray floating in through the windows. The windows are totally open, barred but not screened. The cats freely copulate on the ledge and the stench of their spray practically bursts in on our beds. It's one of the foulest odors I know, the odor of male cat spray.

I thought I was through with cats. During my thirty years of marriage, cats were always a part of our household. One of our most unforgettable ones was George, a tough old un-neutered tom. By the time he was ready to shuffle off his mortal coil, he had sprayed on almost everything we loved, including John's treasured 1911 edition of the Encyclopedia Britannica.

I'm sorry to say we let him roam the neighborhood at night, so he often came home with large gaping wounds, oozing with pus. Once his injuries were so severe I took him to the vet in his cardboard cat carrier that said on the outside: "I'm feeling much better, thanks." He was in such bad shape they had to keep him at the clinic overnight.

The next day, when it was time to pick him up, the temperature hit 20 below. I made John go get him, but he refused to take the cat carrier, said he could easily carry him. When he got to the vet, he was horrified at the bill, reluctantly paid it, then got instructions on how to care for George's wounds that had still not healed. On the way to the car, George lunged out of John's arms and got away down an alley. When John got home he was furious, sputtering about how much the vet's bill was and after all that expense we ended up with no cat. We gave up on George after two days, figuring he'd never survive in that bitter cold with all his little gauze bandages and unhealed sores. But on the third day, he appeared at our back door, hungry and gaunt. He lived on for five more years,

JUNE 9
JOAN

I am really tired today. It rained hard as we arrived in Venice and continued more or less all night. We went out for dinner and got soaked, both by the downpour and the very expensive, not very good restaurant. Then home to a somewhat sleepless night. We were crammed like steerage passengers into our tiny room and even tinier bathroom and the cats came and went at the window all night long. "Let me in" they yowled and when we didn't, punished us with yet another yowl and nauseating spray. We couldn't close the window because it is still so hot here. The rain doesn't seem to cool things off, it just adds to the humidity. It's still raining this morning and we have a full day's agenda planned, with lots of museums.

I hope I can talk Phebe out of part of it. She digs her heels in when I try to skip anything or hurry her along. Especially when it involves culture. She even announced in Paris "Art is my life, Joan." And I always thought her main thrills in life were shopping at discount stores and going out to eat, just like me.

I'm sure I can talk her out of it. Sometimes I'm good at talking her into and out of things. Especially when she thinks it was her idea. Didn't I talk her into getting her ears pierced? I saw an ad in the paper for free piercing if you purchased a pair of gold studs at a local department store. Phebe was scared but I needed the company. For some reason, Phebe went first and when it was my turn I wouldn't do it. "I'm sorry Phebe," I said, "but it occurred to me as I watched you that ear piercing could be called Bodily Mutilation. I'm not going to mutilate my ears." She was livid, wouldn't talk all the way home. Then her ears got infected and she had lots of doctor bills and never got to wear earrings with posts. Weeks later, I finally got mine pierced and had no problem except for Phebe's wrath. But we were still friends.

And we were still friends after the morning at 7 am when Phebe came over and borrowed my husband. She didn't know how to work a helium tank. She had 1000 balloons to blow up, to which she was attaching the 1000 cranes she and one of her peace groups were launching that evening as a remembrance of Hiroshima Day. The very next time I saw my husband was on the 10 pm Nightly News. "Look," my son said, "Look Mommy, there's Daddy!" Indeed there was Daddy, running across the screen releasing balloons.

PHEBE

We're at the Florian Coffee House, a perfect place for us to settle in for a while, a cafe for artists and writers. Goldoni found inspiration for his comedies here, Gozzi for his plays, Guardi for his paintings. Writers from other countries

thought it was a congenial place, too, among them Madame de Stael, Lord Byron, Charles Dickens, Herman Melville, and Marcel Proust. One of our guidebooks said that in two and a half centuries of life, the Florian has become "...the foyer of the most beautiful drawing room in the world: Piazza San Marco."

Joan and I are engaging in one of our favorite sports: people watching and making comments about them as they pass. Sometimes we speculate about their lives. We're sitting safe from the rain under an awning. Most people rush because it's raining, but a young couple just sauntered by, giving up all efforts to protect themselves from the deluge, simply giving over to it, goony smiles on their faces. "Honeymoon couple," Joan said. "No," I countered. "Adulterous lovers."

Here come two men forced to put their arms around each other to stay dry under the same umbrella. Wonder if men in America would risk doing that. They're giggling, too, and acting like kids. I think it's sad that so many men I know don't have close men friends. Often they say their wives are their only friends. I remember John once saying to me he didn't think we needed anyone else, because we had each other. "Let's be a conspiracy against the world," was how he put it. I thought it romantic at the time, but now it seems rather sinister.

An older couple dashes by, the woman with a tiny baby-like fluffy dog tucked under her arm. I ask Joan if I should get myself a dog when I get back home, to keep me company in my lonely hours. "Only if you promise not to dye your hair to match the dog like that woman has!" was her response. She was right. Both of them had the same silvery-blue rinse in their hair.

A young man lopes by with two shopping bags stuffed with purchases and an empty plastic bag arranged over his head to keep off the rain. "There's something we've never thought of, Joan. A folded-up shopping bag would take up very little room in our purses. It would save carrying our umbrellas." The idea horrifies Joan. Our shopping bags are sacred. We carefully save them from city to city. She certainly doesn't warm to the idea of using them as head cover in the rain.

JOAN
(SAN MARCO SQUARE)

Legend has it that Casanova, escaping from his enemies in Venice, couldn't resist the temptation of a last coffee at Florians and so got caught. They've been serving coffee right here since the 17th century.

We're sitting outside, under an awning, listening to the music and eating the smallest sandwich I have ever seen. And the costliest. But we feel a part of the Venetian scene, languid, terribly sophisticated, a tad jaded.

The women going by are so wonderful looking, so well dressed. There are lots of hats. How I envy women who can wear hats. My mother always had wonderful hats but in such up-to-the-moment fashions, they embarrassed me, Now I realize how stylish she was and how proud I should have been of her. No matter what style I try, big picture hats or those little fluffs of feathers and veils, I always look like I'm on my way to a costume party. That goes for anything interesting in clothes, if I'm wearing them. Capes make me look like a Halloween witch, boots like a Nazi general, feathers like Big Bird.

The only thing I ever looked really good in was the strapless formals we wore in the 50's and 60's. From the time I was 13, I had a CHEST. I could Lindy. I could Bunny Hop. That dress wasn't going anywhere.

JUNE 10

PHEBE

In the Doges Palace and I've found a plaque that says "Room of the Four Doors, restored in memory of Ruth Washburn in 1979." Perhaps she's from one of the many old Minneapolis milling families. I think there used to be a Washburn-Crosby milling company that turned into General Mills, our famous business which produced Betty Crocker. Even though many say Betty was only a logo and never existed in real life, I know otherwise. One of my father's few claims to fame, and a small one at that, was that he had met the original Betty Crocker. Her name was Marjorie Husted and she worked for General Mills as a home economist in the nineteen thirties.

A year after my mother died, my father returned to Norway to visit his aging parents. His three congregations had given him the money. We children were farmed out to various farm families. On the USS *Stavangerfjord*, he discovered a familiar name on the passenger list—Marjorie

Husted. Everyone in Minnesota knew that she was Betty Crocker. So he sought her out and found her up in first class. God only knows what she thought of my father's invasion of her privacy. He told the story with great pride for years. I think he even called her up to chat after he'd returned from Norway. Years later, I'm still embarrassed at the thought of it.

Anyhow, whoever Ruth Washburn was, she must have loved Titians and Tintorettos, because here they are in abundance. I'm immediately drawn to Tintoretto's "Mercurio e la Grazie" with its many diaphanous garments. How did he manage to create that gauzy delicacy with oil paints? My guidebook says he was a "tormented spirit" who emphasized voluptuousness in his religious subjects, such as "Suzanna and the Elders."

Much as I'm drawn to Tintoretto, I'm not drawn to writing further about art, even though I've barely begun. So what if I used to insist my students carry their notebooks with them into every museum and gallery they visited. "If you write about the art, you'll see it better," I used to pontificate: "It'll slow you down and you won't merely give a short glance to a work and decide right away if you like it or don't."

Joan seems to have read my mind and has just announced: "The whole city of Venice is a museum. Why not get out of here and simply wander the streets?" Seemed like a good idea to me, so we chucked the Doge's Palace and went out to get lost in Venice's watery streets. While we're wandering about, I tell her my middle-of-the-night revelations about my marriage. "I've made up my mind. When I get home, I'm going to file for divorce." During our walk we kept seeing sundials inscribed with the words: "Horas non numero nisi serenas [I count only the happy hours.]" I asked Joan how I could count the happy hours when I'm about to get a divorce? She answered, "Much of your marriage was happy. You don't have to give up your happy memories."

Why do I keep writing about my failed marriage? It suddenly occurs to me I shouldn't say "failed." Instead I should say it was a marriage that had run its course. Why do I persist in believing marriages have to last for life? Why take "until death do us part" so literally? Why not a re-interpretation? The death of feeling, the death of desire, the death of wanting to be together—those can part a couple as surely as the cold hand of the Grim Reaper.

JOAN

We've walked and walked today all over Venice, across bridges and in and out of little squares, all in the rain which comes and goes. We visited the cathedral and then climbed via elevator to the top of the Campanile or bell tower. While we were up there the bells rang. It was wonderful and unnerving. I thought of Dorothy Sayers and her *Nine Tailors* and could understand it for the first time. Add to the destructive powers of fire and ice, the terrible mind-destroying power of bells.

The Ducal Palace of the Doges was enormous and full of great art. Forty, count them, forty Tintorettos plus too-many-to-count Titians. The ceilings are painted and I would love to be young and limber enough to just lie on the floor and gaze my fill of them. There are acres of statues in huge room after huge room.

I wonder about those Doges. Did they have a grand life in this grand place? As elected officials, they were at the mercy of their Venice neighbors, those who were voters. Many Doges were killed during their reigns and six were blinded by being forced to hang their heads over boiling water.

This gives new meaning to "It's a nice place to visit but I wouldn't want to live there." Better good old suburban Edina. After the palace, I talked Phebe out of another mad dash to yet another museum. After all, this whole ancient city is a museum, I said. Let's just walk about and enjoy it. And so we did. I don't think she's feeling too wonderful today. She was up and down in the night with her stomach pains.

I am also in some pain as I have been bitten all over my body by some strange bugs which I can't see. The bites are horribly itchy and I have scratched the skin off here and there so I don't look too wonderful either. I'm sleeping next to the window and I wonder if I'm not bringing home some interesting Italian fleas from the cats.

Later at dinner at the Trattoria Ponte de Megio: Dinner was wonderful in this charming little neighborhood cafe. Some one told us about it and it was well worth the long walk through Venice's dark and rain-slicked streets. We had antipasto, mixed green salad, agnocotti, fresh filled-pasta, veal marsala and coffee. As we finished, I could feel Phebe's eyes on me and I knew what was coming. Another phrase from our Friend's Shorthand. "My God, " Phebe said, "but we're fat." Years before she had greeted me with these very words as I walked unsuspectingly into her house for coffee. Before this day, she had always told me my excess pounds didn't really show, that I carried them well, or that my clothes hid them. We even wrote the first few chapters of a book on this subject, which we called *How To Be Pleasing Though Plump*. But now Phebe had decided to go on a diet and join a weight management group and she needed a pal to go with her. The gloves were off.

Over the years, either Phebe or I had started many a diet together with those exact same words. I knew the inevitable was near. "OK, " I said. "As soon as we get back to Minnesota, we start another diet."

PHEBE

It's one am and I'm still wide awake, reliving our wonderful evening. We indulged in all the beauties and splendors of Venice at night. We took the vaporetto to a little restaurant tucked away off the Grand Canal. The vaporetto ride was romantic and beautiful. I didn't even have the old yearning I'm so often plagued with to have a man with whom to share the experience. Venice may be a city for lovers—that's what Joan mentioned to me at one point—but I was totally content riding on that vaporetto without one. I gave myself over to the watery exuberance of it, the mist on my face, the lights twinkling on shore. I was totally happy. "Be here now," I kept saying to myself, remembering Ram Dass's advice. I think

I've come to some sort of peace since I announced to Joan I was going to file for divorce as soon as I got home.

The boat ride reminded me of how I loved to go fishing with my father. I have a picture of the two of us in a boat out on the lake near Bagley, Minnesota, the town where I was born. This was when I was an only child, before my interloper brother was born. My father told me to sit perfectly still so as not rock our old wooden rowboat. I loved to trail my hands through the water and watch the ripples my fingers stirred up. My father worried that I would lean too far over the edge of the boat and fall in. We never wore life jackets in those days. I don't remember seeing one until the kapok life vests our men wore in World War II.

At the restaurant we had one of our most superb eating experiences in all of Europe. At first Joan made fun of my ecstatic sighs of pleasure, but soon she was doing it, too. We regaled each other with rapturous descriptions of satiny pasta and exquisitely-spiced sauce. Then I broke the spell by saying we really are getting fat.

JOAN

After dinner, we decided to catch a water bus and ride the canals for awhile as it is still raining out and no fit night to walk. Riding the vaporetto tonight in Venice was the kind of thing that makes all the hard work and frustration of travel worthwhile. We rode in the very front. It was misting slightly and this gave the lights halos and made them seem to float on the water. The night and the soft rain covered up the evil I've felt in Venice.

Maybe it's the chill, the never-ending damp of this place. You sense that parts of Venice never see the sun, that damp has crept into these marble palazzos and for century after century filled them with mildew, with rot.

My feelings also come partially from the little history I know of Venice, of their awful politics, even to selling out allies and the Church during the Crusades for a few lire. The guidebook says the Renaissance people of Venice were noted for being self-centered, self-protective, dedicated only to having a good time. It seems incredible that such grasping, greedy sorts should have created this fairy-tale city.

And it is a fairy tale come true tonight. As we walk through San Marco Square and back to our hotel, I listen for the sounds of nights gone by. Whispers. The soft slither of a velvet cape, just ahead, turning a corner, the faintest strains of a minuet, a smothered laugh. Mysterious, wonderful, romantic Venice.

Perhaps the only people to see Venice clearly are lovers, so you should come here only when you are incredibly, breathlessly in love. Then you would see only the perfect beauty and be blind to the evil which hangs just below the romance in this soft Venice air. I make a solemn vow to come back here with Bob and see Venice blindly, perfectly.

PHEBE

Late at night in our hotel, I am interrupted in my writing by the sound of Joan's voice. She moaned, half sat up in bed, moaned again and said, "What? What?" Then she fell back to sleep. I remember when we were young mothers, drinking coffee together while we watched our children play, Joan would sometimes look at me and say, "What oh what's to become of us?" That question always took me aback. Why did she ask it? Did she think life was passing me by? Was staying home with my kids and tending to house and husband not enough?

Every time she asked that question, I felt stricken. I thought the question implied that my life were somehow meaningless. After all, she was working outside the home but I wasn't. Now I realize that I did the best I could during those years, despite my anxiety and depression and panic attacks. I'm finally learning not to worry so much about the future, but to take each day as it comes. As my father would say, "Sufficient unto the day is the evil thereof."

So dear Joan, if the "What? What?" you're murmuring in your sleep has to do with that old question, "What oh what's to become of us?" I'd like to answer you, "We don't know what's to become of us. There's no point in worrying about it anymore. The now is all that matters. This is what has become of us and there's still lots more ahead." One of the few things I've learned as I grow older is to value every experience, to understand that despite all the mistakes I've made and wrong turns I've taken, this is my life and it is good. I could wake up Joan and share my terrific life philosophy. But I've learned to let sleeping Joans lie.

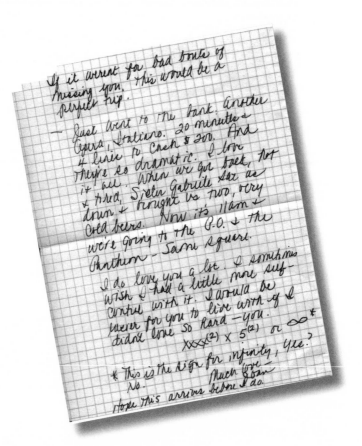

11. CLIMBING THE DOLOMITES
Digging for roots

JUNE 11

JOAN
(CARCIATO, ITALY)

On the train to the Dolomites: We're on a trip today to look for my roots in the town where Mom's parents were born. I tried to find my family once years ago. I was in Milan and asked for a ticket to Carciato, a little town in the Dolomites, the Alps of Northern Italy. I knew from my mother's stories that both my Grandmother and Grandfather Stanchina were born there. The man in the train station looked and looked in his books and couldn't find it. He tried to convince me that I was wrong, that Carciato didn't exist. I knew it did but I couldn't prove it, couldn't spell it, couldn't even remember the names of the towns around it.

I remember today how sad I was then not to be able to find it. My mother was old and so forgetful that I felt I had already almost lost her. Now I was losing part of her again and part of my history too.

After my parents died, I was cleaning out the house where they'd lived for 40 years and I found a journal Mom had kept on her Grand Tour of Europe in 1925. There, in her own words and her dear, familiar hand-writing, she told me how to get to Carciato:

"Carciato, Val de Sole (Valley of the Sun)

Leave Venice 11:30pm, Arrive Trento 2:47 pm

Change trains and stations in Trento. Leave Trento 4 pm and arrive Male 5:30 pm.

Took a cab from Male to Dimaro. Uncle Bortolo met me in Dimaro and we walked across a little stream to his home in Carciato."

Phebe and I are trying to follow Mom's journal entry to the letter today. It has worked perfectly so far and we're on a train almost to Male at the moment. The trip up here was so beautiful. We started into the Alps about an hour out of Venice and the higher we climbed, the more I felt I belonged. After changing trains and stations in Trento, this little mountain goat of a train is climbing up to Male. It's heaven up here. Pines and carpets of Alpine flowers. Rushing streams coming straight down from the top of the mountains, high bridges over deep, carved-in-the-rock rivers. Tiny towns, red-roofed and pastel-hued clinging to the earth and seeming to climb the mountains.

We stepped off the train into a town so perfect it's like a Hollywood stage set for an enchanting mountain town, in Technicolor. There are two hotels right where the cog railway ends, one buttercup yellow and one rose brown. We chose the yellow one with the great green shutters. There are flowers everywhere, great banks of them in long boxes on the outside of the hotel. The air is crystal and cold with just the faintest smell of wood fires. There are enormous pine trees, the ground under them covered with cones and needles.

The woman at the desk of the hotel seemed formal and unapproachable until I asked her if she happened to know of an Anna Stanchina, the cousin who I was told, lives somewhere near here and speaks English. "I know her well, very well," she said. "Your cousin is married now, her name is Anna Stanchina Fantelli and she is Vice Director of the tourism bureau for the whole area, the

Val di Sol." Then she called my cousin for me. "Don't take a cab to Carciato. Your cousin wants to come for you this evening. She has her tennis lesson after supper, then she will be here."

I knew that things would be different here, no longer the sleepy little town my grandparents had left, a town where they took the cattle up into the mountains in the summer. Now it's a famous ski resort where you can ski all year round. I don't know what I expected but not this, a woman cousin in Italy with a high-powered career, one that has regular private tennis lessons. I am nervous waiting for her.

I love this hotel. We have the biggest room we've had on the trip with a carved armoire for our clothes, great feathery beds and huge windows looking out on the mountains that surround us. After we unpack, we go for a walk before dinner and stumble into a little store selling cards and books. The women there are so nice and very curious. They get few American tourists in this part of Italy. When they find out my mother was a Stanchina, they're very excited and tell me that I have many, many cousins in the Val di Sole.

We go in to dinner in the hotel and the owner comes up with an Italian/English dictionary and says, "Now we'll have a laugh." So we do and struggle together to order the best dinner of the trip. It starts out with a thick soup which she has called Dumplings Tyrol and which is, YES, Kilindery. I haven't had this soup since my Mother died. It was a tradition, a monthly offering throughout my childhood. I start to weep to the dismay of the poor waitress. She calls the owner back and I try to explain to her why I'm crying. Oh, how I wish Mom knew I was here. Why did I never tell her how good this soup is? It took her all day to make it.

Evening in the Alps: I can't believe my cousin Anna's kindness. After working all day and then playing tennis, she came for us at 9:30 and took us to her sister Virginia's home in Carciato. It's darling and so are my cousins. We have a great time although Virginia doesn't speak English, nor do Phebe and I speak Italian. Anna, a consummate professional, speaks fluent English, German, French, and a little bit of several other languages. How I envy her.

Virginia is the elder, she's not married, and works most of the year in a neighboring ski resort but is home now for the summer.

Her house is wonderful, with lots of wood walls, an open floor plan, a cozy fireplace and a bedroom loft with a fur bedspread. She is five years younger than I am, and much smaller, with bright blue eyes and light brown hair.

Anna is tiny with dark hair and huge brown eyes, quick moving and very sophisticated. She is eight years younger than Virginia. We look at family pictures, write our family tree, exchange family myths and gossip.

It's hard getting to sleep, I'm so full of ghosts tonight. I can hear my mother and her five sisters, sitting around the dining room table after a big family dinner, talking in Italian. My sister and I ignored them, never asked if we could learn. We were from an Irish neighborhood so Pat and I with our red hair, freckled faces and tomboy interests fit right in. Whenever anyone asked us what nationality we were, we yelled IRISH. My father, the sweetest and gentlest man that ever lived, loved it, would throw back his head and roar with laughter. Of course, we identified with my father. He thought we were perfect, laughed at everything we did, never said a cross word to either of us. My mother was the disciplinarian.

Mom was formal, private, a proud woman of great moral and intellectual integrity. She had been a junior high school principal, expected great things of us, and taught us, by example, all a woman could do, could be. She was my rock, it never occurred to me that I would have to go on without her. I get up and open the shutters and look out on the sleeping mountains. I wish with all of my heart that my mother knows that I am here, knows that I am still looking for her.

PHEBE

Here we are in Male, near Carciato, where Joan's grandparents came from. I was quite surprised when Joan said to me a few days ago, "Have I got a treat for you!" I'm wary whenever she begins a sentence with that. Years ago, when she first said it to me, it turned out the "treat" was going to her nephew's graduation ceremony a hundred miles from Minneapolis. Her own husband wouldn't go with her, so I was pressed into service. I had to spend the evening talking to strangers, including a mink rancher who talked endlessly about the mating habits of his little animals.

This time the "treat" was that we'd deviate from our carefully-planned schedule and go visit her Italian relatives in the Dolomites. At first I was upset. She had refused to go to Norway with me to visit my relatives. That had been the whole point of my original trip. Now she was asking me to take a detour to visit her Italian relatives.

Furthermore, I hadn't known she had Italian relatives. All the thirty years I'd known Joan, she emphasized only her Irish roots, even keeping her Irish maiden name, Murphy. "You have relatives in Italy? First I've heard of it. I thought of you as Irish to the bone."

I reminded her of how she loved to talk at parties about the hardships her ancestors endured during the potato famine and how no other national literature had produced greatness such as that of Yeats and Synge and Joyce.

She immediately took umbrage. "You haven't been listening to me. I've talked about my mother's Italian relatives as long as you've known me." Maybe I hadn't been listening to her because I was jealous. I've always wished for a few hot-blooded Italians among my forebears. Even John turned out to be not all Norwegian and Swedish. When his mother came to live with us once, she started talking to me about her childhood.

I'd always believed she was 100 percent Swedish and proud of it. She had grown up speaking Swedish in her home. After she got married, she carried on all the Swedish traditions. Then one day she told me her great secret. "You know, my mother was Swedish, but my father wasn't. He was born in Rumania of a gypsy family and migrated to Sweden when he was a little boy. After he married my mother, they emigrated to America. I remember he wore an earring and I was embarrassed by that. None of the farmers around Alexandria, Minnesota, wore earrings!" My mother-in-law wasn't the typical blonde blue-eyed Swede. She was dark-skinned, black-haired, and prided herself on being able to stay out in the sun all day without getting burned.

But then my father didn't look like most people's idea of a Norwegian either. He too had black hair and what he used to call a "Roman nose." Maybe he had gypsy blood as well. He was certainly adventurous, the only one of his family to come to America. Often he would tell us how he made the decision after being struck down by the Spanish flu. He was choking on his phlegm and the doctor had to perform a kitchen-table tracheotomy. "God saved my life. That's why I decided to become a minister. It was a close call. You might never have been born." During my snotty adolescence, I liked to point out it was the doctor, not God who saved him.

JUNE 12
JOAN

I didn't sleep much last night. I am going to meet relatives, touch lives that I didn't know existed and yet are a part of mine. We decide to meet early as we must leave today and there are many relatives who Anna says will be offended if I don't meet them, and she wants to take us first up into the mountains to see the skiers.

When Anna picks us up, we go first to her office in Male to check train times. The road between Dimaro-Carciato and Male will close at 12:15 for a big national bike race. We must be back then in four hours.

We pick up Virginia and meet my cousin Elena. I would have known she was my cousin without being told, she looks so much like my aunt, one of mother's sisters. She is delighted to see me, "cugina, cugina." She remembers being huge with child and someone said to her, "You'll have twins like your cousins in America." My mother was one of those twins. She grabs my hands and kisses me on both cheeks, when we meet, when we part.

They all do that. Anna did as soon as we met. They shake hands with Phebe and then kiss me twice. They are completely accepting, seem so happy I'm here at last, that I've found them. It feels so strange. It feels so right.

We go next to my grandfather's boyhood home, owned by Stanchinas for 400 years. Virginia and Anna each own part as do two cousins who live in Milan and use their apartments for vacations. Grandpa's home is an incredible structure, four or five stories high, immense. Each floor has a long corridor going straight through with doors to apartments opening off it. Over the years it's been mainly a family home with the bottom floor for the cattle and farm supplies. Now some of the space has been modernized, some is still the way it was in the 1500's with great, enamel stoves for heating in each room. One upper floor was used as a prison during World War I for over a hundred Czechoslovakian prisoners

Virginia brings out huge boxes of family photographs, my great-grandparents, dead cousins, aunts and uncles. We sit outdoors in the sun, in front of mountains that seem as familiar and dear to me as the lakes of Minnesota. There is a huge picture of my mother's family, all eleven children and her parents, in their Sunday best. They had it taken for mom's grandparents, still living in Carciato. And there are bundles of letters from my mother to her cousins, Anna and Virginia's father and aunt. It's a shock to see my mother's handwriting. I'm amazed they've saved all of her letters over the years. I remember so clearly the days she would write them. Surrounded by her old college textbooks and an Italian-English dictionary, it would often take her all day long to finish a letter in Italian to her satisfaction. I hold one of her letters, written in 1947, to my cheek and feel so blessedly close to her.

We visit Zia (Aunt) Speranza next for coffee and a little grappa. She is small and round, apple-cheeked with a bun of white hair. She keeps touching me, patting my cheek, holding my hand. Her son Giovanni, young and handsome lives with her. The house is wonderful and very old, entered under an arch, through a great courtyard with a barn on one side. While we're there, there's a sharp knocking on the door and shrill cries. It's the gypsies they tell us, demanding money that Zia Speranza hurries to get. Funny, I didn't know Italy had gypsies.

It appears to break Zia Speranza's heart when we have to leave so soon. I hate saying goodbye to her too. She is so warm and lovable. We go on to visit the church, built in the 1500's, where I know my grandparents were baptized and my great-grandparents married, baptized and buried. How many more generations of my family I wonder. Isn't it funny I wasn't baptized here? I feel as though I could or should have been.

Next we go to my cousin Guiseppi and his wife Luiga. More wine in an incredibly beautiful house. On the outside, it's obviously ancient. You go under an arch, cross a little private bridge over a rapidly running mountain stream, into their courtyard. Inside, everything has been completely modernized. Guiseppi, has done all this work himself. Downstairs, in a separate apartment, we visit his sister, Cousin Maddelena, a tiny, energetic woman with huge, soft, sweet eyes. She insists on sharing with us yet another bottle of wine. It's a local favorite she tells us and it is delicious, a fruity, dry white wine.

We talk and talk so long that Anna is nervous. She's afraid the bicyclists will be here sooner than expected, the roads closed. So we have to leave. Again, my cousins hug and kiss me and again I fight back tears at their openness, friendship.

Anna and Virginia take us back to the hotel. We must pack quickly to go back down the mountain. It has been the most full to overflowing, compressed twenty hours of my life. I feel now as though I have roots, ones that go right into my heart. When the train comes, I promise Virginia that I will come back and that I will learn some Italian so that we can talk. Anna says, "Come and live here for awhile, I will find you an apartment. " It's so hard to say goodbye to them. "Will you write?" Anna says again and again.

12. OUR WATCH ON THE RHINE
Germany by bus and boat

JUNE 12
PHEBE
(ON THE TRAIN TO MUNICH)

Visiting Joan's relatives turned out to be a moving experience for me, too. They took me in as if I were one of them. I began to believe I too was Italian. I felt especially close to Anna, who showed us her new home in the new village. It was near the old Carciato, now occupied as Anna said, "mostly by old people." In the US we'd probably tear down the old village, but here in the land of Joan's forebears they have the good sense to hang on to their old buildings

Anna and her husband have a prosperous, very modern life. They're a two-car family, their son Matteo has a computer, their house is impeccable and beautifully decorated. Anna showed us her photo albums. As she turned the pages, I had the curious sensation of being part of their family. She dwelled on each picture, always identifying everyone by name and giving a few descriptive sentences for each one. Anna's mother died when Anna was a baby and she stayed with relatives. That made me feel even closer to her.

Such an odd feeling, turning the pages of the photo albums so quickly. Whole lives went speeding by—christenings, birthday parties, first communions, picnics at the beach. A photo of her on holiday with her English boyfriend. ("It didn't work out so we parted.") Later, photos of her with her fiance, now her husband, the wedding, the birth of Matteo— whole albums devoted to him. We must have seen six or seven albums in the short time we were there. Like those movies that speed up the process of a flower budding, then opening to fullness before your very eyes.

My own cousins in Norway are much on my mind now. Ester, who's exactly my age, is the one I feel closest to. When I was in Norway as a student, she and I became good friends. Once we visited Vigeland Park together in Oslo. A sunny day, many families with their children trying to climb the statues, all those wonderful statues of babies and young children and adolescents and their mothers and fathers and grandparents, all intertwined together in tall columns. Ester put her arm around me, something I was not used to. In Norway, young girls often walked around together with their arms linked. There were tears in her eyes. "Even though we meet for the first time, I feel so close to you, as if we were sisters." She said it in Norwegian, but I understood her and my eyes filled with tears, too. Then she added, "Do you want to have children some day?"

It was the furthest thing from my mind then. I was trying to avoid "going all the way" with my Norwegian boyfriend because I had a dread of getting pregnant. In 1950 I knew nothing about birth control devices, probably wouldn't have been able to acquire any if I had. I told her I didn't really have a boyfriend yet, but I knew I wanted to get married someday. And yes, I guess I wanted to have children although I hadn't given it much thought. "I'll have to find someone to marry first!" I said.

JOAN

Depression settled over us like a maggoty, raggedy blanket on the train for Munich. I had spent so much time the past day with my relatives, swallowing hard and wiping away the tears that my eyes were red-rimmed and gummy and my voice hoarse. Besides which, I'm sure Phebe and I were both a little hung over. "A few more days with my relatives," I told her, "and they'd have to put us in treatment when we got back to Minnesota. In about four hours, we helped put away three bottles of wine plus the grappa in our coffee."

I know my sadness was also over leaving la bella Italia for Germany. Smugly, I have always wondered about people with prejudices, wondered what kind of people they were, who could fear other people, simply because of the color of their skin, where they were born, or their sexual orientation. It is a little humbling to realize that I have harbored fear and dislike for Germans since childhood.

I was in first grade when World War II started and although I don't remember being terrified for the next four years, I must have been, because those years are burned so strongly into my memory. Our next-door neighbor, Mrs. Cohen, said that the Germans wanted to melt her down into a bar of soap. I loved Mrs. Cohen, she was so beautiful with a great bun of pure white hair. It scared me to think of her being hurt. Or my own dear Uncle Rudy. My mother said he was safe, it couldn't happen in America but I wasn't sure. Hadn't Uncle Rudy been fired, along with all the other Jews, from a department store in St. Paul?

It was right during the Depression and he and Aunt Rose had to come to live with us while he looked for another job. Then they had to move out of town to find work and I didn't get to see them nearly as much. So I knew bad things could happen to people I loved.

Now here I am in Germany for the first time and the train is crowded, hot and dirty and there are people jammed into the aisles. They won't move, even when we say "fehr-sigh-ung" again and again which someone has assured us means "I'm sorry." So we have to push and pull and drag our bags right over them.

Finally, we get to the only compartment that has two empty seats. It also has the rudest woman I've ever met. She has put her purse and packages on one of the empty seats and has her feet up on the other. We stand there saying "fehr-sigh-ung" again and again while she ignores us. Finally, I put my bag under the seat, moving her feet slightly as I do it. Then I pick up her purse and hand it to her. At long last she looks at us, saying snottily over and over, "Just a moment please, just a moment please" as she slowly, slowly removes her packages from the second seat.

The train ride today seems never ending. It's very hot and the rude woman has turned the heat on full blast even when we ask her to turn it down, even when we fan ourselves vigorously with magazines bleating piteously SAHARA, SAHARA. Up and down goes the window to the corridor. We open it, she gets up and, leaning right on us, closes it again. Now she is trying to see what I'm writing in my journal. BITCH. BITCH. BITCH. This is for you, lady.

PHEBE

There's a woman sitting across from me with a very expensive-looking straw purse, with Velcro closings, which she opens and closes with great briskness and with unnecessary frequency. I wince each time the Velcro pollutes the air with its annoying harsh sound. I could get behind the cause of outlawing Velcro or at least making it a crime to open and close it in public.

Velcro Woman has gotten off the train, thank God. Joan and I are alone in our compartment. We've eaten our sandwiches and passed through Innsbruck. Joan is asleep, once again missing all the gorgeous snow-covered mountain scenery. I refuse to take any naps. As our trip nears its end, I'm determined to stay awake except for the few hours I have to spend in bed when it's dark. When I get to Norway, it will be light all the time.

I remember when I was there in the summer of 1950 how painful it was to sit with relatives who didn't speak English through the endless summer evenings, straining to hear and understand every word. Because they didn't want to miss the wonderful light, they stayed up most of the night. I was exhausted. Finally, I learned to say one phrase in perfect Norwegian and it will probably come in handy this time around: "I must go lie down now."

As we entered the suburbs of Munich. I saw a McDonald's sign flash by and then came that absurd sense of pride. I must be getting homesick for my country, when fast food signs fill me with pride. I've always loved fast food places and have often attacked people who criticize them. I think they're part of America's greatness.

When we arrive I fall into a deep depression, feeling utter despair about the human race, distrusting every German I see, my age or older, holding them responsible for the Holocaust. Has any nation ever done anything quite as horrible as what the Nazis did in the camps? Joan reminds me of what the English did to the Irish, of what we did to the American Indians, of what the Japanese did to the Chinese, of what the Chinese communists did to their own peasants. So everyone is guilty.

My despair lasted far into the evening. I decided it would be just as well for the whole human race to end. My natural optimism faded and I found it hard to sleep. I want to cast my lot with faith, in spite of the world's evil, but sometimes in the middle of the night, horrible thoughts overwhelm me.

I had wanted to love Munich, the city Rolf had been so happy in during his junior year abroad. I had wanted to be enchanted by this city and be able to share my experiences with him when I returned. The summer after he got back from Munich, he and I drove up to the North Shore of Lake Superior. We sat together on the rocks outside my cabin, while he read aloud to me from his journal. I felt so close to him then, completely caught up in his experiences while I listened to him. I'd never wanted to go to Germany myself, but because he loved it so much, I was slowly getting over my aversion. How unfair of me to castigate a whole country. I hated to hear that Europeans blamed all of us for the Vietnam

War's horrors, especially since I'd been opposed to that involvement.

Writing about Rolf makes me homesick. Home. But where is home now? I don't feel I have a home anymore. My parents are dead. I can't go home to them. My marriage is dead. I can't go home where John still lives. I have moments, despite all the work with my therapist, that I fantasize myself driving over to my old house in the middle of the night, quietly slipping into bed beside John. In my fantasy, he embraces me and says what he once said after we reconciled following an argument and a long silence: "It's so good to hold you in my arms again."

Then reality strikes. That isn't my home any more. What if I found him in bed with another woman? What makes me think he has any desire to take me back? And once again, the hard question: Do I really want to go back?

But the strong feeling that I have no home persists. My apartment seems like a temporary dwelling. Would I feel more at home if I bought my own place? Sometimes I drive past the old house and imagine that the life we lived, back in the 60's when the kids were little, is still going on inside. If I were to enter, I'd still find us all there, happy, and serenely unaware of what lay ahead—misery, alienation, brokenness.

JOAN

Phebe Talks Tough. "There were these Italians at the shop trying to get ahead of me, with handfuls of that cheap souvenir crap. I just threw my body in front of them. I heard one say "signora!" in a shocked voice but I didn't care. They clearly were in the wrong.

"Then I made the sales lady mad. I said I want a bag and she said you mean rucksack and I said yes, just to humor her. When she got it down I said no, not that kind, get me that one up there and she said, well, madam that's a bag not a rucksack and I said well, that's what I asked for in the first place, isn't it? Then I made her go look in the storeroom for a black one. She claimed all she had was lime green."

Later, proudly carrying her new BLACK bag, Phebe tried to buy some antacid in another store. The lady spoke no English so Phebe attempted to show her in mime what she needed. Her dramatic, silent portrayal of a heartburn sufferer very nearly killed the clerk who reeled back into the corner, pale, with her hand on her heart. When she realized Phebe wasn't about to die right there in her store, she pushed us out the door muttering, "Apotheke, apotheke".

We walked all over old Munich this afternoon and evening, attempting to just get the flavor of this city. After a wonderful German dinner, we headed for the hotel and an early night to gird ourselves for a tough day at Dachau tomorrow.

JUNE 13

PHEBE
(DACHAU)

Joan and I agreed to go our separate ways here because we wanted to be silent. I followed a little path into the woods behind the crematorium where I found wooden markers, each one labeled carefully: "Gallows Stand," "Grave of Unknown," "Ash Grove," "Pistol Range," "Execution Range with Blood Ditch," "Grave of Many Thousands Unknown," and "Ashes Were Stored Here." Some of the markers have flowers planted around them in neat stiff beds.

I have wandered around the desolate grounds, through the museum, into the auditorium for a documentary film, then along the empty spaces where only foundations stand, filled with pebbles where the prison houses once were. Four memorial chapels at the end of this row. The Dachau memorial wasn't put in place until 1965.

Last night I dreamed about my friend from Augsburg, who served in the US army in Germany and was present at the opening of one of the death camps. When he returned to resume his education at Augsburg, his old German professor called him into his office and said, "Was it really true?" When Sam said yes, he had seen it with his own eyes, the professor fell silent. Then he began to weep.

JOAN

Before we are allowed out into the camp itself, we are herded into a movie. The film jumps around, seems non-committal and terribly non-emotional. And isn't that one of the things that this place is all about, to allow us to release some of our emotions about the Holocaust?

Next we are shown into an exhibition hall with huge pictures of life in the camp. I am overcome, can look no more, when I see a picture of a child looking scared. Somehow the photos of piles and piles of bodies are almost too horrible to believe. But the picture of one little boy in terror, being taken from the Warsaw Ghetto, is unbearable. "Plus Jamais"—Never Again— the theme of a French sculpture in the camp.

There is a huge map with lights showing the main concentration camps and dots on the map and a list of the subsidiary camps that fed each awful place. The map covers all of Germany and its occupied territories. Where did they get all the workers for these camps? And how could they not have known what was going on?

When we sign the guest book, we notice that the majority of the names and addresses are American. Some Canadians. Some French and other European countries. I turn back the pages and read as many as I can before the guard stops me. Very few names and addresses from Germany. Perhaps they don't sign the book when they visit. Outside, the camp seems cleaned up for company. Even the three churches here are cold, modern, stark. The actual prison dormitories are gone, in their places are neat rectangles of dirt and stone.

There are signs telling you not to bring children under ten but there are several family groups here today with children that young and younger. And young people with backpacks. Is this a summer outing?

Ahead of me two Frenchmen argue loudly about numbers. Logistics perhaps of the terrible efficiency that went on here. Why are they here? Why am I? For forgiveness perhaps. One of the exhibits tells me that 3000 Catholic priests were imprisoned and most died here. Would I have the courage? If not, do I have the right to hate those who did this or allowed it to happen? Can I forgive? I must because hatred cannot go on, generation after generation. It must stop and I want it to stop with me.

The lilacs are just about to bloom outside the crematorium. Inside it smells bad, like gas, and looks clean, very efficient. Someone has put a votive light inside one oven, a lighted candle stub inside another.

I wish I had brought flowers or a candle or something. Anything.

JUNE 14

PHEBE
(MUNICH)

We have been trying to decide whether to go on the Romantic Road tour or not. I feel we should plunge ahead with our plans. "After all," I point out to Joan, "you made these plans in the first place. I never wanted to go to Germany."

She ignores that comment. "I'm afraid we won't get to Amsterdam in time for me to catch my plane if we take both the Romantic Road tour and the boat trip up the Rhine." I want to point out if we hadn't taken the time out to see her relatives in Male, we wouldn't have to worry about getting to Amsterdam in time.

I do understand her anxiety, having suffered from it many times myself. So I try to be patient with her. "All right," I say, "let's take the train this afternoon to Rothenburg, since that's the town on the Romantic Road we both most want to see, then a train directly from there in the afternoon to Wiesbaden. We'll be there in plenty of time for the boat out of Wiesbaden on Tuesday morning."

I feel I've been very willing to go along with a change in plans, even though sometimes I seethe inside. I'd love to talk her out of her anxiety, but it's futile. She'll have none of my patient explanations about how we can easily do everything we'd planned and still get back to Amsterdam in time. She gets up and walks away from me.

"You aren't listening to me. You don't understand what I'm trying to say. I'm going out for a walk." Finally, she reconsiders, apologizes for being so cross, and we end up deciding to take our chances tomorrow of getting seats on the Romantic Road bus tour. Then we walk together around Munich for a few hours. It is a beautiful city and now I understand a little better why Rolf loved it.

JUNE 15
JOAN
(ROMANTISCHE STRASSE)

As part of our Eurail Pass, we're allowed the Romantic Road bus tour. As it goes North from Munich to Frankfurt, we decided to take it. We imagined that the bus will be crowded with tourists taking advantage of this Eurail plus. So we got to the bus station early, dressed in our finest. When we asked the man at the counter if he spoke English, he was startled. "Why, you're Americans," he said. "I thought you were from the Balkans. The babushkas, you know. And all your little plastic bags."

This was very nearly the final straw for Phebe who has been fretting about the paucity and dullness of our outfits for weeks. I am actually relieved that our outfits have hidden our American roots, as I have forgotten nearly all the Norwegian that Phebe so patiently taught me before we left. That was to be our second line of defense against anti-American terrorists. We would pretend to be Norsk. The only thing I can remember at this point is 'Et oy blick' which means in the blink of an eye or in a moment. Phebe thought this might be enough. She would chatter away smartly in Norwegian, I was to throw in an occasional "yah", "nay" or "et oy blick" and we would be home safe.

We're going through amazing medieval towns with stops in four of them. Augsburg, a Roman village for 500 years, now has a walled city within for poor, married Catholics of good reputation. So few Western Germans meet the poverty qualifications now, there are always apartments available for 1.50 marks, which is less than a dollar per year.

Outside Augsburg, we go past a frightening thing called the Elephant's Cage, an enormous wire cage ringed with lethal-looking missiles. It's part of an American early warning system.

Donauworth on the Danube has a bridge that has been destroyed by floods or war 30 times. I think I'd give up rebuilding the damn thing after the first five bridges.

Nordlingen. From the church steeple here, if it's a clear day, you can see 60 other steeples. If steeples are your thing, Nordlingen is clearly your town.

Dinkilsbuhl and a stop for two hours. We had lunch at the Golden Hind, established 1405. People live in houses here and all along the Romantic Road that would be covered in glass or put into a museum in the USA. These are fairy tale cities and towns, perfectly preserved. War doesn't seem to have ever come here. Illness did, though. There's a large memorial thanking God for ending the plague and delivering the Dinkilsbuhls from the Black Death. Outside of town, a road sign points to "Hellenbach, 1 k".

Rothenburg ob der Tauber is said to be the most perfectly preserved medieval town in the world. It is completely shut in with ancient walls that we attempted to walk all the way around.

Wurtzberg. Mozart played here in a room lit by 11,000 candles, if I understood the guide. Seems like an awful lot of candles. Where would you find enough people to get them all lit before the first ones died out?

Somewhere along our bus trip, Phebe decides that all roads in Germany must lead to Ausfahrt. She says, "I've seen signs for it everywhere today. It must be the biggest town in Germany and I've never even heard of it." After our little dustup over Senso Unico in Rome, I'm a little afraid to speak up and tell her that Ausfahrt is just the German way of saying EXIT on a highway.

PHEBE

As we entered the outskirts of a town, I saw an old woman, wearing a purple wool midriff jacket, with long puffed sleeves and the predictable peasant's kerchief. She was dragging two huge sacks. "Maybe she lives in one of those shacks," I said to

Joan. "Odd to see slums on the edge of town. Usually they're in the inner city." Joan then pointed out to me that people don't live in these shacks. "These are garden plots for people who live elsewhere. Those shacks are tool sheds."

As we drove out of town, a woman leaned out of an ancient house. "There's Edna St. Vincent Millay and she's waving at us!" "Can't be," Joan said, without looking up from her journal. "She's dead." "No, she's not. She's alive and well and starting a new life along the Romantic Road, a perfect relocation for her, I must say." I started to wave back at Edna, but it was too late for her to see me, so I dropped my hand. "Was Dorothy Lamour standing next to her?" Joan asked.

Now we are crossing the 49th latitude, according to our guide. Should we feel the difference? I feel like a child again, on a field trip bus, with a guide who makes announcements and hands out information sheets. Yet it's comforting too.

We've had our lunch in Dinkelsbuhl, another jewel of a town. Brilliant flowers in the town square like the ones in Grand Marais. I saw a Snickers wrapper on the sidewalk and had an insane desire to pick it up and smell it. My favorite candy bar. Made me homesick. I've never seen one in a store here. Some Snickers lover carried it in her suitcase all the way to Germany.

JOAN
(WIESBADEN)

When we got off the bus at Frankfurt's Main Bahnhof, it was late and we were sure we had missed our train to Wiesbaden. But, what a surprise— an efficient German train, that's 30 minutes late! Again things work out slick for us. A fast train to Wiesbaden and then a cab to the suburb, Biebrech, where we will catch the boat tomorrow for a trip up the Rhine. Our hotel is across the street from the boat dock so we have a view of the river. It's tiny but it has a good bed and a brand new bath.

Phebe and I had our first serious argument tonight. She kept insisting that I had said I was a rich woman since my father had died last fall and left me some money. I reacted so strongly, it scared me. I know it scared Phebe too, because she didn't say another word about it all night and was unusually soft-spoken.

At first I thought it was the idea that dear old man had to die so I could inherit his money, a guilt most children who love their parents share. Now I realize my anger hides my fear. I've been pretending on this trip that Dad is still alive, that he'll be there when I get home.

He was always so glad to see me, so interested in what I was doing, where I had been. I haven't been able to face the fact that he's gone. No one will ever love me that unconditionally again. Is anyone ever really ready to be an orphan?

What do you do with all your left-over love and loyalty when a person dies? I can't bear to throw away even one picture or momento even though our little house is choking on books, pictures, paper. When I throw away dad's yearbook or mom's prom cards, I feel I'm losing a part of their lives. If I throw too much away, they'll disappear forever.

It was hard giving away dad's clothes but I did it fast, the first week after he died. He didn't have that much left, refusing nearly all my offers of shopping for him or with him. He did buy a new suit a few months before he died. As the man measured him, Dad said comfortably, "This will be a nice suit to be laid out in."

I wouldn't talk to him about death then or ever that last year. And he wanted to talk about dying. On Memorial Day, we had a picnic on our deck and when Bob went into the house for a minute, dad announced, "You know dear, I've had this strong feeling. I think I'll be dying soon, in the next few months."

The Murphy family have always treated death casually, a little like emigrating to a New Land, one you might return from as often as the spirit moved you. Family history was full of the ghostly appearances of Uncle Joe or Grandma Connolly, who came back often just to say howdy or to stop a member of the family from doing something silly, like Marrying Outside The Faith.

Whenever and wherever Murphys gathered, there were always tales of fresh sightings of our dearly dead and departed. Settling in cozily, Cousin Patrick would talk about seeing Uncle Tom, dead ten years, at Mass that morning. Or Aunt Mary would retell Grandma's deathbed sighting of her mother, Great-Grandma Mary. Sitting bolt upright in bed, Grandma said, "Mother! How good of you to come for me. And who is that with you?" There was always much speculation at this point of just who the Second Spirit was on the day of Grandma's death.

I've been told all my life that I have inherited Second Sight from both Grandma Murphy and Grandma Stanchina which I always felt was a doubly terrible gift. "Leave me your pearls or diamonds when you go," I've begged every member of my family. "I do not want to inherit friendly little chats with the dead. Please, please do not ever appear to me after you die."

So I just couldn't talk to my father about his death; I didn't want to believe in his omens. Furious with fear, I told him, "I'm not going to sit here and listen to that Irish Catholic premonition crap, Dad."

Instead we talked about the yard and how much Creeping Charley we were getting under the fence from the neighbors and how warm it was for a day in May. He died five months later and I missed my chance of talking to him about his death and my death. I wish I could tell him that a lot of my fear went away with him. I'm not so afraid of death anymore.

PHEBE

We took a train after we got off the bus in Frankfurt, called the hotel from the railroad station and found a room. We were offered a choice of room with bathroom down the hall or bath in the room. I wanted to save money and was willing to go down the hall.

I got my way, but Joan wasn't happy. We're reverting to childish behavior again. "I'm cold," Joan just said. "My coverlet isn't as thick as yours." "Put your silk underwear on," I said. "I don't know where it is, and it's your turn to get up and turn the light off so why don't you get it for me?" Since I had to go to the bathroom anyway, I agreed.

As we near the end of our trip, I'm not the only one obsessively counting money. I want to make sure I have enough to last me through Norway. But now even Joan has been worrying out loud about all the money she's spent on this trip. Then I made a big mistake. I said to her, "Oh, you're not really worried, are you? You said to me after your father died that you were a rich woman now."

She got furious. "I did not. I never said that." "Yes, you did. I clearly remember that you said: 'I'm a rich woman now but I'd rather have my father back.'" But she was adamant. "I never did. I never said that. You really hurt my feelings. I don't want to hear another word about it."

So I shut up, knowing I'd crossed some very big line. We've argued all the time on this trip, but we've never been really mad at each other. This anger is different from any other I've seen her show before. After what seemed like an endlessly long silence, we talked of other things. Then we both drifted into sleep.

JUNE 16

JOAN

The ship is coming in now and it's wonderful. Four decks high with flags flying and music playing. On board, there are many restaurants and lots of tables to sit at and write in our journals, both indoors and out. It will take us from 9 am to 2 pm to float up the river from Wiesbaden to Koblenz, the stretch of the Rhine, we're told, with the most old towns and castles. The Rhine seems as wide as the Mississippi, where it flows through Minneapolis, and a whole lot busier.

Every other square foot of the hills that rise sharply from the water are covered with grapevines for—what else? Rhine wine. Trains run along the banks on both sides of the river but I think this boat is the best, laziest way to really see the Rhine. We just passed the Mouse Tower, so named because it sits right down on the shore of the Rhine, watched over by its castle on the hill above, the way a cat watches a mouse.

Our boat is loaded with darling German children, about 10-12 years old, all speaking English and all wanting to try it out on us. "What's your name, how old are you, where are you from, is that near Chicago?" Although Minneapolis is a good 400 miles from Chicago, I have taken to answering 'yes' to that question. It saves having to draw a map of the USA for foreigners who have never heard of Minneapolis or Minnesota for that matter. I love these kids, they're fun without being fresh and their English pronunciation is pretty darn good.

Phebe has gone up on the top deck of the boat and way out in front where it's too cold for me. I'm glad to be alone for awhile, I want to think quietly about my life back home and write in my journal. I'd like to be able to write about my father today. My sister and I had worried that he would have to move when my mother died. He was then 91 years old. But one by one, our children, his five grandchildren, moved in and lived happily with him, so he was never left alone.

He was a part of their lives without ever being judgmental, unfailingly supportive without trying to control them. At ninety-four, he was still open to new ideas, amazingly free of self-pity or complaints and always adaptable. With one grandson, he had seven months of take-out Mexican dinners, as neither one of them could cook much and a Taco Bell was on the grandson's way home. Another granddaughter came with a friend and a cat and left them both behind when she moved to Europe. No matter. My dad adopted the friend, learned to live with the cat. I can't stand to think he won't be there when I get home. I can't think about it any more today.

This has felt like a day that's twice as long as the days at home and I think that's because I allow myself very little "free' time at home. I am so busy, busy that I've taken to using four colors of ink on the calendar in the kitchen so that I won't forget anything. Part of that busy-ness is a left-over teenage need to be popular. See how many friends I have? See how many social engagements and meetings and jobs I can crowd into one month?

Part of it is that I don't always want a lot of time to think about my life. On this trip, like the tongue going to a canker sore, I go back again and again to the failures. The lost friends. The end of my first marriage. Merry's suicide which I might have prevented if I'd been smarter. All the things I didn't do for Dennis, all the times I neglected my parents. With enough time, I can conjure up a hill of Sins of Omission that I can't see over.

I wanted to be a saint but I'm not. I was determined to be perfect mother but I was too selfish. And I always wanted to have a marriage just like my parents, and I didn't with the first and I don't with the second either. I can never remember my parents fighting, I can't even remember any harsh words between them. I'm sure they must have disagreed but when they did, they kept us out of it.

Someone told me it isn't good for kids to grow up without conflict but I can't think why. What good does it do kids to hear parents ranting and raving? Mom would occasionally go into her room and close the door or sit alone out on the front steps in the summer. That was her idea of a Big Fight. To be honest, I'm not sure my Dad even knew she was upset.

Standing by the open grave on the day of my mother's funeral, I saw my father reach out and pat the coffin. The priest noticed it too. He asked him gently, "How long were you and Anne married Murph?"

"Fifty-six years," my father said." We were married fifty-six years."

"Of course," Monsignor Dillon said, "I remember coming to dinner when we celebrated your Golden Anniversary."

"It was always golden," my father said. "Every year. It was all golden."

PHEBE

So here I am on a sunny June morning floating down the Rhine surrounded by laughing and chattering school children. A wave of nostalgia comes over me as I remember last summer when I took my creative writing students down the Mississippi on a big paddle-wheeler. Seems like a tame trip compared to this. But for German kids the Rhine is like our Mississippi. I'm happy to be floating down the Rhine.

My good mood doesn't last long. As I settle in for what seems like an endless trip, I start to wonder why I didn't remember how boring river trips can be. I ask myself where is the peace and contentment I experienced in Venice? There I decided I could live a complete life as a single woman. I was so at peace then with my decision to file for divorce.

Do other divorced women feel this same hopelessness over being mateless and homeless? Sometimes I wonder why I went to all the trouble to search for a mate—and it was plenty of trouble, because John read a lot of Kierkegard and agonized over whether he should even get married. Actually, what's so great about always doing things as a couple? Most of the years I was married, I engaged in an ongoing struggle to get John to go to dinner parties or concerts or plays with other couples. He wanted just the two of us to go by ourselves. Much less trouble, he always said.

An American couple here on the deck have all four of their small children with them, including twins of about a year old. The little boy is wearing a Harvard sweatshirt. Why didn't they buy a Harvard sweatshirt for his twin sister? Is she not destined to go to Harvard? The other two children are about two and four. Their parents are holding hands as they sit side by side in their deck chairs, overseeing their children. One of the little boys has just snuggled into his own deck chair to suck his thumb and rub the satin binding on his blanket. The little girl is on Mommy's lap.

I remember a snapshot of our family standing in front of our VW bus the summer we were at Deer Lake Family Camp. We look tanned and healthy and happy. But when I look more closely, as I often do because the picture stands on my bedside table, I notice John's arm is around mine, squeezing it, as if he's trying to keep me in the circle. I do look like I want to escape. I'm leaning just a bit away from him. That fall I went back to the U, got my teaching certificate renewed, learned to drive, got a teaching job and changed all our lives.

I just saw a stork in a little canal alongside the railroad tracks and remembered one of Erik's favorite childhood books, *Wheel on the Roof* by Meindert de Jong, about the return of storks to Holland every year. I've written so much about my childhood and my kids' childhoods on this trip. I've thought of them often, but I haven't worried about them in the futile way I often do back home. Of course the worrying never goes away once and for all. Years ago a friend who'd been married for five years told me she and her husband were trying to decide whether or not to have a child. "Such a big commitment. Eighteen years out of our lives." I laughed. "What do you mean, eighteen years? Once your child is born, your life is changed forever. You never draw a worry-free breath again. "

13. FULL CIRCLE TO SCHIPHOL
Saying goodbye in Holland

JUNE 17

JOAN
(AMSTERDAM)

It seemed like home here, a funny sensation as we came into the train station that was so foreign and scary just a few weeks ago. There were all the same sad junkies shooting up and sniffing powder all over the place. Now we just feel the pity, the fear is gone. We have become bold and seasoned, traveling through the cities of the Continent.

We went back to the hotel where we started except now they know us and have saved us a wonderful room right on the Herengracht Canal. And what a room! Huge windows all across the front looking out at the bustling street scene and the canal with its ancient buildings across the water. Crystal chandeliers. Color television. And an enormous, private bath. Deluxe beyond dreaming for our last day in Europe.

After a wonderful dinner, we got cleaned up and repacked for home for me and Norway for Phebe. We went through our clothes carefully and Phebe chose some of my outfits to take to Norway with which she hoped to impress her stylish Norsk cousins.

"They'll impress them, all right," I told her, "but not the way you think. They'll probably give you things from their own closets, they'll feel so sorry for you." After six weeks of daily wear, all my clothes have that bad garage sale look, overworn and overwashed. Phebe made me try on everything I own, at least twice, and very solemnly chose an outfit for me that she guaranteed will make me irresistible to Bob tomorrow. I said how can the very same clothes that were so drab people thought we were from the Balkans miraculously change into sexy duds?

We took a very long time over our toilette tonight and watched "Hill Street Blues" on TV as we creamed our faces, washed and curled our hair, attending carefully even to our toenails. No telling what Bob or Phebe's cousins will notice. We laughed a lot and then got sad, thinking of parting tomorrow, our trip together over.

We read bits of our journals to each other and were amazed to find that our entries were as much about what we had left behind at home as they were about all the new things we'd experienced in Europe.

I told Phebe I was happy we'd waited to go on the Grand Tour until our fifties. Older women have more life to draw on for understanding and enjoying new things. I never would have believed this when I was 20. Now I consider 50 to be a midpoint— are you listening, God?—and a perfect time to stretch into unknown places while I think about my first half-century and plan where I'm going for the next half.

JUNE 18

PHEBE
(ON THE TRAIN TO COPENHAGEN)

While Joan and I were waiting for my train, we began to talk with a couple who were also taking the train to Copenhagen. I think Joan decided it would be good for me to know someone since I would now be alone. She thinks I need her care, even though she's the younger. She's right, too. I will be lost without her.

Anyhow, this couple, who are Americans, are also going to Oslo. He's quite a bit older, very wrinkled. Her face is carefully made up, so her skin looks flawless, almost mask-like. And her hair is well-sprayed. No breeze could ruffle it. "We're in Europe for the fourth time," she tells us. "I've seen enough of Italy now. I don't care if I ever go to Italy again. Actually, we wouldn't have come this year if we hadn't been invited to Rome for the ordination of the son of a friend of ours."

Both Joan and I had been put off by her jabbering up to this point, especially as she kept referring to her husband as "the mister" and bragging about all he'd bought for her on their trip. She even pulled out of her purse a gorgeous ensemble— necklace, bracelet, and earrings—clear crystal alternating with emerald green. "With a black dress, won't they be lovely?"

Soon the train came and there was no way out of it. Joan and I had to say goodbye. I reassured her I'd be all right even though I didn't think I could remember a word of Norwegian. So many people in Copenhagen and Oslo speak English.

Now I'm alone. I waved and waved to her, until her figure grew fainter and fainter, in its beautifully-tailored and carefully-fitted bone raincoat. Bone, the other color we so deliberately selected back in America to keep us inconspicuous. She had tied a tasteful wool challis scarf so perfectly over her auburn hair. As I watched her disappear, I realized how exquisitely she was dressed. Never had she looked so cosmopolitan, so utterly the sophisticated world traveler. Her figure grew tinier and tinier and my eyes watered until I could see her no more.

Yes, I am alone, speeding backward in a train to Copenhagen, the sky beyond my window leaden and overcast to match my desolate mood. Chilly here in this compartment. A young woman has joined me and I am so relieved to have her presence. She won't want to talk to me because she is reading what appears to be a manuscript. Now she's reached into her plastic bag for a red pen to make notations. I'm colder than I've ever been in all of Europe, but she seems to be warm so there's no chance of enlisting her aid in getting some heat in here.

I don't believe I have any more Dutch money, but I cleverly cadged a few bits of food from the breakfast bread basket back at the Hotel Ambassade when Joan wasn't looking—cheese and ham and two slices of wonderful dark bread. So I'll survive until I can change traveler's checks to money in Copenhagen. Much as I hated our decision to never spend more than $50 on any given day, it did keep me from dipping ahead into money I'll need in Norway.

I've actually taken the initiative to move into another compartment which is much warmer. The couple Joan and I met on the station platform are here and I'm amazingly happy to see them. They're from El Paso. This is the second marriage for both and they've been "happily married" for eight years. Between them they have eight children and ten grandchildren.

She's working on getting an annulment of her first marriage so they can be married in the church. She wants a BIG WEDDING with long white gown and all the kids as attendants. Her priest is helping her apply for the annulment. He suggested it and agreed to help her answer the questions on the FOURTEEN pages of forms. "It costs $250 but it's worth it. I don't mind making that kind of contribution to the church."

They're comfortable to be with, have great quantities of food with them, which they freely offer to me, first delicious mixed nuts coated with a salty-sugary glaze. She is insistent that I take more. "Here, that's not enough. Pour some in this glass. There. That's more like it." Later they break out a bag of prunes and offer me some, giggling like teenagers. "If these don't work, we have Ex-Lax, too!" I decline the prunes, but they munch away happily.

Then he goes down the aisle and comes back with two cans of soda. "Let's save one of these so we can mix it later with our liquor." She giggles. "We like to carry a few bottles with us. We like to have fun. In the eight years we've been married, we've mostly traveled the whole time. Have you ever been on a CRUISE? They're the most fun of all."

A strange peace settles over me as I listen to them babble on to each other. I'm being blessed with one of those moments that come to me far too rarely, like some sort of grace, without warning, but with a great rush of happiness. I'm contented just to watch my pen move steadily across the lines of my little blue journal, bought in the stationery store in Male.

I'm suddenly very thirsty. They didn't think to buy me a can of pop. After all, why should they? Just because I was starting to feel like their grownup child? When the minibar man comes through, I remember my little legacy from darling friend and companion of the last happy weeks. Even though she's at this very moment being hurled through space across the Atlantic and back to Bob, yet she is with me.

Back in Amsterdam, Joan had pressed five Deutsch marks into my hand. "You might need these on the train if you get thirsty." So I buy a Pepsi with three of them and raise the can to Joan and our unforgettable weeks together. Then I drink deep, watering the bread and cheese from Amsterdam and the nuts from El Paso and fall asleep as the train slips into Denmark.

JOAN
(FLYING HOME)

Saying goodbye was so strange. It seemed all wrong for Phebe to be climbing on a train and going off without me. She got on and put the window down in her compartment so we could talk but all we could say was—"It's over, it's over, wasn't it all wonderful, the best trip any two people ever had, you are my dear friend, I am going to miss you so." We both cried a bit, then we waved and waved and waved, with Phebe hanging out the window farther and farther as her train went around a curve and out of sight. And there I was, alone in Amsterdam.

The Martinair flight home was wonderful. Until we hit Chicago, of course. They poked and prodded us all through customs here. Why are some U.S. Customs people so unfriendly? What a first impression of America for foreign visitors. The young people all get really searched, they must feel everyone under 30 is on drugs. They rolled me right out the door, didn't even look in my suitcase. I look way too bland and respectable.

Middle-aged women can get by with anything, I've decided. Unless they know you, people don't really look at you anymore when you're of a certain age. Too old to be sexy, too young to be a character. Good, gray matrons. We could smuggle elephants into the country and they'd never notice.

The plane is late, hope Bob isn't waiting out at the airport. I did tell him to call. How will Bob act, what will he say? Will we be foreign and strange with one another? I'm very messy even though I'm wearing what Phebe assured me is my "best" outfit. Pink cotton pants, black tank top and plaid overblouse, large brown shoes with gum soles. Both arms scarred from Venice bugs. Straight-as-a-stick hair. Red-rimmed eyes, dry, cracked lips. Bob might take one look and go home without me.

Well, if he does I guess I'll live through it. I certainly won't like it but one thing I'm determined to be is more independent. My moods too often hinge on Bob's moods, how I spend my time is largely determined by how Bob wants to spend his. I know this isn't good for either of us. I've taken a big step by getting out of the agency. Now I've got to keep climbing, keep figuring out what I want to do with my life, keep growing.

I don't know. I think sometimes I've spent my whole adult life worrying about whether or not there was a man in it. Feeling happy when there was, sad when I didn't have anyone. Was I going to be chosen during Spin the Bottle in sixth grade? Would I be asked to the Prom? Was I going to be an Old Maid? Well, there usually was a man and looking back I don't think it was this fact that made me happy or sad. When I was happy, I was happy with the man in my life too. Seems so clear now but it was a hard thing to learn. I do like men, that's true. But I like the friendship and company of women too. And I quite like my own company.

After saying all this, I still find myself breathless with anticipation, a little like waiting for that first kiss, first prom date. I can't wait to see Bob, wish I could get out and push the plane down the runway and up into the air.

To pass the time, I go though all the little odds and ends in my carry-on bag—the brochures and tickets and maps and postcards and timetables and new friend's names scratched on little scraps of paper—and they all seem so wonderful to me, so evocative of this city or that day. This napkin reminds me of the smell of bread baking first thing in the morning in Paris, the sand still stuck to my sunglasses, of the hot sun on the beach in Italy, the matches of the glowing candles in front of the Virgin at the Villa Rosa.

I hold them one by one in my hands and ponder what the last weeks have meant to me. Like the shards of pots and pieces of bones that archeologists put together to recreate a long-disappeared civilization. I know that if I could put together all these bits and pieces I've saved from this trip, I could recreate it, preserve it in my memory as clearly as I remember whole years of my childhood.

I certainly will never forget the big moments—the privilege of seeing great things with my own eyes, the peace of living in a convent, the joy of finding my relatives, the time and distance to examine my life. Phebe was right to make me write it all down. This journal will always be proof that the two of us had the courage to travel our own way, without guides or someone to carry our bags or rigid schedules or lots of money. We traveled not-so-fast and not-so-rich and not-so-young through Europe and we had the grandest of all Grand Tours.